# Divine Release: Unleashing Spiritual Prosperity

Prophetess Dr. Monica B. Kearse

Copyright © 2015 Prophetess Dr. Monica B. Kearse.

All rights reserved. No part of this book may be used or reproduced by any means, graphic, electronic, or mechanical, including photocopying, recording, taping or by any information storage retrieval system without the written permission of the publisher except in the case of brief quotations embodied in critical articles and reviews.

Photographer: Lauryn Kearse

WestBow Press books may be ordered through booksellers or by contacting:

WestBow Press
A Division of Thomas Nelson & Zondervan
1663 Liberty Drive
Bloomington, IN 47403
www.westbowpress.com
1 (866) 928-1240

Because of the dynamic nature of the Internet, any web addresses or links contained in this book may have changed since publication and may no longer be valid. The views expressed in this work are solely those of the author and do not necessarily reflect the views of the publisher, and the publisher hereby disclaims any responsibility for them.

Any people depicted in stock imagery provided by Thinkstock are models,
and such images are being used for illustrative purposes only.
Certain stock imagery © Thinkstock.

ISBN: 978-1-4908-6857-8 (sc)
ISBN: 978-1-4908-6858-5 (e)

Library of Congress Control Number: 2015901839

Print information available on the last page.

WestBow Press rev. date: 03/04/2015

# CONTENTS

# INTRODUCTION

### The Unprofitable Servant: Faith and Duty (Luke 17:8-10)

*"And will not rather say unto him, Make ready wherewith I may sup, and gird thyself, and serve me, till I have eaten and drunken; and afterward thou shalt eat and drink? Doth he thank that servant because he did the things that were commanded him? I trow not. So likewise ye, when ye shall have done all those things which are commanded you, say, 'We are unprofitable servants: we have done that which was our duty to do."*

As the Lord instructed me to write these sayings, He reminded me that it was not for me but for others who would benefit from hearing real life situations. He told me, "When you have done all the things commanded of you say, 'I am an unprofitable servant. I have done what was my duty to do.' "Prepare the fields and I'll supply the rain," says the Lord. "Go out into the highways and byways and make My way straight and noticeable. I want all men, women, boys, and girls to know that I AM LORD. Your first assignment will be in a small group setting. People will come from all walks of life. Your role will be the Prophetess, Dr. Monica Bennett Kearse. Once you have spoken My Word, do not forget to honor Me in all that you do, and I will lead the way. I will make provisions for you and your household. There will be no lack. Write the vision and make it plain according to My Word, and I will provide the resources. All the things that you speak, seek, teach, and touch in My Name will be blessed. So remain humble, abstain from pride, and watch the glory of the Lord come in. Wherever your feet trod will be blessed. Gird your loins, and stay in My face, and watch My glory be manifested before you. Do not be afraid, but "seek ye first the kingdom of God, and His righteousness, and all these things shall be added unto you" (Matthew 6:33). The time is nigh, and all the things that you have hoped for are coming to pass. Everything that you have dreamed about will be manifested in God's holy and matchless name. Do not fear. Doors are getting ready to open that no man can shut. Take the ride! Give God glory! Give

Him honor and praise in Jesus' name! I decree and declare it in the mighty name of Jesus! Hallelujah!"

Everything should be done for the building up of the Kingdom. Our duty here on earth is to fulfill the needs of the lost, the babes, and the unknown. We are to go out into the highways and byways to meet the needs of others. There are people all around us who desire to know the Lord, in prison and in unfamiliar places, looking for attention and spiritual guidance. Instead of overlooking them and saying negative things, give them a word from the Lord. "Then shall the King say unto them on His right hand, Come, ye blessed of My Father, inherit the kingdom prepared for you from the foundation of the world: For I was an hungered, and ye gave Me meat; I was thirsty, and ye gave Me drink; I was a stranger, and ye took Me in; naked, and ye clothed Me. I was sick, and ye visited Me; I was in prison, and ye came unto Me. Then shall the righteous answer Him, saying, Lord, when saw we Thee an hungered, and fed Thee? Or thirsty, and gave Thee drink? When saw we Thee a stranger, and took Thee in? Or naked, and clothed Thee? Or when saw we Thee sick, or in prison, and came unto Thee? And the King shall answer and say unto them, 'Verily I say unto you, inasmuch as ye have done it unto one of the least of these My brethren, ye have done it unto Me" (Matthew 25: 34-40). "I know thy works; behold, I have set before thee an open door, and no man can shut it, for thou hast a little strength, and hast kept My word, and hast not denied My name" (Revelation 3:8).

I have accepted my assignment and the journey that has been placed before me. I heard a whisper, and I followed His command. As you read these passages of scriptures, place yourself in them, and write your thoughts of what you would do. This is good reading for Bible studies and gatherings. Everyone may not be able to identify with each passage, but I am sure something will fit your situation or circumstance. Join me, and others, in making God's word come to life for people everywhere.

## LESSON 1

# *Preparing for a Divine Release*

**Foundation: 2 Peter 1:1-8**

*"Simon Peter, a servant and an apostle of Jesus Christ, to them that have obtained like precious faith with us through the righteousness of God and our Savior Jesus Christ: grace and peace be multiplied unto you through the knowledge of God, and of Jesus our Lord, according as His divine power hath given unto us all things that pertain unto life and godliness through the knowledge of Him that hath called us to glory and virtue. Whereby are given unto us exceeding great and precious promises; that by these ye might be partakers of the divine nature, having escaped the corruption that is in the world through lust. And beside this, giving all diligence, add to your faith virtue; and to virtue knowledge; and to knowledge temperance; and to temperance patience; and to patience godliness; and to godliness brotherly kindness; and to brotherly kindness charity. For if these things be in you, and abound, they make you that ye shall neither be barren nor unfruitful in the knowledge of our Lord Jesus Christ."*

### A. Conquering the Spirit of Doubt

Do you have days when you think God is ignoring the desires of your heart, the things you want out of life? Do you sometimes wonder why things are going so wrong when you are trying to make it right? God denied your request because He has something far greater in store for you! The righteous have to go through trials and tribulations. The faith of the righteous says, "Nevertheless, not my will but Your will be done." "O my Father, if it be possible, let this cup pass from me: nevertheless, not as I will, but as thou wilt." (Matthew

26:39). You do not know how it is going to turn out; it is only by God's will. You feel a sense of surrender to fail and die within. You shall not die, but live to declare the glory of God (Psalm 118:17). When the spirit of doubt comes to you and says, "Quit! Give up! You can't do it!" You rise up and tell that spirit, "I don't think so! I'm righteous and a child of the Most High God! I am blessed, highly favored, and deeply loved. I can do all things through Christ which strengtheneth me" (Philippians 4:13). When you seek Christ and ask Him for that which is necessary for your life, He will give you the desires of your heart. Ask the Lord to give you the power to fast, to pray, to heal, to apply the blood, and to speak His word. You cannot be stagnant; you must keep working for the Kingdom. You must persevere. You are responsible for using your spiritual prosperity to heal the nation.

### B. Spiritual Prosperity Does Not Come Easy–Seek God First

"But seek ye first the Kingdom of God, and His righteousness; and all these things shall be added unto you" (Matthew 6:33). Do just that: seek Him first. He wants you to get it right with Him, and He will release the rest. Spiritual prosperity does not come easy. It will increase with due diligence and faith adhering to the word of God. You must be willing to keep your eyes on the Kingdom and not quit. "For the Lord God is a sun and shield; the Lord will give grace and glory. No good thing will He withhold from them that walk uprightly" (Psalm 84:11). The Lord knows all about those things that concern you. That which is divinely given is the only way you can divinely release. You are trying to work it in the natural, trying to fix it. You become irritable and tired because you are trying to fix it carnally. When God gives you something, a spiritual gift, you've got to release it! When the power of God overtakes you, you will have the unction to release it! The higher you go in God, the more He will divinely release spiritual blessings. It comes with righteousness. It is something that happens to you when you hear from God. It triggers your spiritual being and brings to remembrance that He gave His only begotten Son to save His people from their sins. That was a release from God to man. "For God so loved the world that He gave His only begotten Son, that whosoever believeth in Him should not perish, but have everlasting life" (John 3:16). The next thing God does in your life will have to be divine, or it will not happen. If you are not aligned with the will of God and things become disarrayed, remember that you made the mess; so, deal with it. Instead of wallowing in your mess continuously, just release your life to God and allow Him to make you the person He ordained for you to be. It's a challenge going through the daily struggles of life on your own. Why not submit to God? If you don't submit to God, you will eventually submit to something. Step out on faith and seek God.

## C. Faith is the Substance

Once you seek Him and align your life with His will, things are going to be multiplied. He will give you prosperity, freedom, anointing power, ministry, passions, gifts, and the things that you desire that are in His will; just have faith. Faith will begin to turn your situations around, and you will begin to see things multiply. "Now faith is the substance of things hoped for, the evidence of things not seen" (Hebrews 11:1). Everything you have believed God for will be multiplied. Sick bodies will be healed. When you release your praise, you are divinely releasing God's deliverance. Something that may take years to flourish will immediately begin to come out when the spirit of the Divine steps in. When you hear the prophetic word, you are delivered by grace immediately. The divine release today is by an immediate discharge of deliverance and freedom. The power of God will overtake you. Something is getting ready to change. You are walking into your destiny of deliverance: victory over cancer, sickness, disease and death. It is your time to release! Sow a seed to a ministry or somewhere where God can get the glory, honor, and praise. Become sharers and partakers of His divine nature. "According as His divine power hath given unto us all things that pertain unto life and godliness, through the knowledge of Him that hath called us to glory and virtue. Whereby are given unto us exceeding great and precious promises; that by these ye might be partakers of the divine nature, having escaped the corruption that is in the world through lust" (2 Peter 1:3, 4).

## D. Hidden Treasure of Giving

The Bible speaks of men and of women who were born of, moved by, compelled by, and impelled from God to be a blessing to others. It is the divine nature of God that He asks us for something. "For where your treasure is, there will your heart be also" (Matthew 6:21). Let the Lord know that you trust Him more than your possessions. Tell that devil, "YOU'LL NEVER TRICK ME AGAIN. RELEASE ME BY THE POWER OF JESUS CHRIST. I COMMAND YOU, SATAN, GO BACK TO THE PIT OF HELL WHERE YOU BELONG." Speak with authority to the devil. Convince yourself of God's authority over your life. What about people in this country and other countries who are in need? It is time to become a partaker of the nature of God for them. Your last seed is your favor seed. When you are down to your last, in a financial deficit, just know that the seed that you have in your hands is your seed. It is your seed of favor. His divine power can take this seed and multiply it. "There is that maketh himself rich, yet hath nothing; there is that maketh himself poor, yet hath great riches. Wealth gotten by vanity shall be diminished, but He that gathereth by labor shall increase" (Proverbs 13:7, 11).

Jesus taught obedience by the things that He rendered. When you have tried everything else, and you do not have the means to make ends meet, go back to believing miracles. The only thing that pleases God is when you move by faith and trust in Him. "But without faith it is impossible to please Him; for he that cometh to God must believe that He is, and that He is a rewarder of them that diligently seek Him" (Hebrews 11:6). When you give something that is precious to you, God will divinely release more to you. When the divine release breaks forth, it will be a season of miracles and praise. It will not be a one-time thing. You will begin to have favor on your life, for the Lord is married to you. No more shall you follow the dictates of your evil hearts. Call God "my Father," and do not turn away from Him. Return to God – put away your abominations out of His sight; then, you shall not be moved. Obey the voice of our God. "And the Lord smelled a sweet savor; and the Lord said in His heart, I will not again curse the ground any more for man's sake; for the imagination of man's heart is evil from His youth; neither will I again smite any more everything living, as I have done. While the earth remaineth, seedtime and harvest, cold and heat, summer and winter, and day and night shall not cease" (Genesis 8:21, 22). See also Matthew 13:45, 46.

**E. Seek God's Righteousness**

"Whosoever abideth in Him sinneth not; whosoever sinneth hath not seen Him, neither known Him" (1 John 3:6). Let God lead and guide your thought process. If it is not in His will, it will fail or shall not come to pass. Once you die to the flesh and allow the Holy Spirit free reign in your life, then you will begin to see the manifestation of God's grace go into effect. Let Him have free course to do what He pleases, and watch the exposé of the Holy Spirit have its way. Take up your cross and follow Him. "Then said Jesus, unto His disciples, 'If any man will come after Me, let him deny himself, and take up his cross, and follow Me. For whosoever will save his life shall lose it; and whosoever will lose his life for My sake shall find it. For what is a man profited, if He shall gain the whole world, and lose His own soul? Or what shall a man give in exchange for His soul? For the Son of Man shall come in the glory of His Father with His angels; and then He shall reward every man according to his works. Verily I say unto you, there be some standing here, which shall not taste of death, till they see the Son of man coming in His kingdom'" (Matthew 16:24-28).

What are your works? What have you done and are still doing for the Kingdom? God wants us to give our lives to Him and for Him. God desires for us to live a Kingdom-minded life where He is the center of our lives. Once we allow the worries and cares of this world to consume us, we forget about the ultimate being that is responsible for our very existence. We must live a fulfilling life where the pleasures are given to seek God first. Where are your treasures, and what is consuming your thoughts? Are you fulfilling your true destiny in life? Are you allowing the desires of your heart to overwhelm you, and you have forgotten about the Kingdom? Is there a pleasure in life that can benefit the elect ones in your life? Have you done a good deed where God can get the glory? Is it self-fulfillment or Kingdom riches? Will you lose your life for it? Will it benefit the Kingdom or is it selfish indulgence? "The pride of thine heart hath deceived Thee, thou that dwellest in the clefts of the rock, whose habitation is high; that saith in His heart, 'Who shall bring me down to the ground?' Though thou exalt thyself as the eagle, and though thou set thy nest among the stars, thence will I bring Thee down, saith the Lord" (Obadiah 1:3-4).

What will your reward be according to your works? Even when you have backslidden, God is still faithful. When things are grim and seems like the weight of the world are on your shoulders, He is still faithful, and He is just. God will sustain and lead you. "If we confess our sins, He is faithful and just to forgive us our sins, and to cleanse us from all unrighteousness" (1 John 1:9). Once you put your trust in Him, He will see you through. Sometimes our darkest hour is subject to failure and disappointments on every hand; that is when He is strong. He is forever faithful to keep us when we are weak and cannot control the things crumbling around us. Keep your eyes on the prize and watch God do the rest. "Therefore I take pleasure in infirmities, in reproaches, in necessities, in persecutions, in distresses for Christ's sake; for when I am weak, then am I strong" (2 Corinthians 12:10). Let Him lead and guide your thoughts. If it is not in His will, it will fail and shall not come to pass. Once you die to the flesh and allow the Holy Spirit to reign free in your life then you will begin to see the manifestations go into effect. Let Him have free course to do what He pleases, and watch the manifestation of the Holy Spirit have its way. Allow God's grace to take control of your life. "For we are the circumcision, which worship God in the spirit, and rejoice in Christ Jesus, and have no confidence in the flesh. Though I might also have confidence in the flesh. If any other man thinketh that He hath whereof He might trust in the flesh, I more. But what things were gain to me, those I counted loss for Christ" (Philippians 3:3-4, 7).

**F. Remember Your First Love**

God does not want us to turn away from our first Love – He is our first Love. "Nevertheless I have somewhat against Thee, because thou hast left thy first love" (Revelation 2:4). We cannot forget Him because He has not forgotten us. Even when you are at your darkest hour or feel like nobody cares, that is when He is forever faithful to send you a reminder that His mind is stayed on you. Keep your head up my sister or my brother. When the road seems like it is running out, He will stretch it out even more for you to understand and feel His presence. What are you thinking that is so fretful that you would want to give up and want to give in? What is so bad in life that you cannot see your way through it? Return to God, and He will show you a better way. He will put abominations out of your sight. Break up the fallow ground and sow new seeds of spiritual fruitfulness. "But grow in grace, and in the knowledge of our Lord and Savior Jesus Christ. To Him be glory, both now and forever. Amen" (2 Peter 3:18).

**Discussion Questions:**

1. **Do you feel like giving up when things are not going your way? What do you do to change it?**

2. **Does life sometimes seem complicated and pointless? Do you change the situation or yourself?**

3. **Do you often think there has to be a better way in life? Do you make the necessary changes for the "better" to occur? Why or why not?**

4. **Do you seek God for your decisions? Why or why not?**

5. **Explain how you feel like there is a hidden treasure inside of you.**

6. **Are you ready to be activated to do things His way or will you continue to do them your way? Explain.**

7. **Can you put aside the ill feelings you have towards others and pick up the love of Christ even for your enemy or a person you know does not like you? Explain.**

**Points to Discuss: After reading the lesson, go back and answer the questions in the lesson for an in-depth discussion.**

**Notes:**

# LESSON 2

# *For His Glory*

**Foundation: Romans 3:12**

*"They are all gone out of the way, they are together become unprofitable; there is none that doeth good, no, not one."*

## A. Follow God, Not the World

Look to the hills from which cometh our help. All of our help comes from God. Seek the Lord now while He may be found. Search the scriptures for direction and leadership. When you seek God with your whole heart, He will show Himself to you. God wants your undivided attention to see what He can and will do in your life. Just when it seems like the whole world is in chaos all around you, this is the time that God wants you to know that He is in control and will allow you to see Him in the midst of the storm. Read Psalm 46:1-3. Do not turn to the left or the right. Do not look at the world's circumstances, but look at God's spiritual provisions for your life. When things seem crazy and out of control, you are to follow the order and direction of God to complete an assignment. Remember, God will not allow more to be placed on you than you can bear. "There hath no temptation taken you but such as is common to man; but God is faithful, who will not suffer you to be tempted above that ye are able; but will with the temptation also make a way to escape, that ye may be able to bear it" (1 Corinthians 10:13).

He has a blessing for you but you must tap into His holy chambers. Once you have encountered Christ, you will never be the same. In the book of John, Jesus met the Samaritan woman at the well. "Jesus answered and said unto her, 'Whosoever drinketh of this water shall thirst again: But whosoever drinketh of the water that I shall give him shall never thirst, but the water that I shall give him shall be in him a well of water springing up into everlasting life'" (John 4:13-14). "God is a Spirit, and they that worship Him must worship Him in spirit and in truth" (John 4:24). "FOR WHO HATH KNOWN THE MIND OF THE LORD? OR WHO HATH BEEN HIS COUNSELOR? OR WHO HATH FIRST GIVEN TO HIM, AND IT SHALL BE RECOMPENSED UNTO HIM AGAIN? For of Him, and through Him, and to Him, are all things, to whom be glory forever. Amen" (Romans 11:34-36). God has all power in His hands. The earth is the Lord's and the fullness thereof. "There shall be no lack and doing without in the latter days," says the Lord. Rumors and discredit will be ruined. They shall be cast down and put to shame in my name. Do not fret or have second thoughts, but put on the whole armor of God, and you will be able to stand against the wiles of the devil." A second chance is all everybody wants. Prepare the way and God will do the rest. "Finally, my brethren, be strong in the Lord, and in the power of His might. Put on the whole armor of God, that ye may be able to stand against the wiles of the devil" (Ephesians 6:10, 11).

## B. No Pain, No Gain

Suffering had to take place in order to bring you to this level. Because of a little suffering, the reward is even greater. Search the scriptures, and you will see where Jesus suffered much for our sins. He died so that we might have life and have it more abundantly. "The thief cometh not, but for to steal, and to kill, and to destroy; I am come that they might have life, and that they might have it more abundantly" (John 10:10). All glory is given to God. "Verily, verily, I say unto you, he that heareth My word, and believeth on Him that sent Me, hath everlasting life and shall not come into condemnation but is passed from death unto life. Verily, verily, I say unto you, the hour is coming, and now is, when the dead shall hear the voice of the son of God: and they that hear shall live" (John 5:24,25). The sacrifice is the same when you do it in Jesus' name. It is worth it. No pain, no gain. "For it became Him, for whom are all things, and by whom are all things, in bringing many sons unto glory, to make the Captain of their salvation perfect through sufferings" (Hebrews 2:10). "Now the God of peace, that brought again from the dead our Lord Jesus, that great Shepherd of the sheep, through the blood of the everlasting covenant, make you perfect in every good work to do His will, working in you that which is well-pleasing in His sight, through Jesus Christ; to whom be glory forever and ever. Amen" (Hebrews 13:20, 21). Have you, or has someone you know, lost weight? Surely this person exercised in a disciplined manner for health reasons or just to feel better. Whatever the reason may be, it was a sacrifice. No pain, no gain. In order for you to see better results, you have to commit to doing better things in your life. In order for circumstances and situations to improve there has to be something you give up doing or something you change to make a difference. Try doing something positive that is out of the ordinary, and watch God get the glory through your life.

### C. Preparation for His Glory

God was making and preparing you to be complete to do His will. He was molding you into His image so that you could have a testimony to hear and tell others about Christ. All glory belongs to God. He is working in you to do His will. "For whosoever shall do the will of God, the same is My brother, and My sister, and My mother" (Mark 3:35). Count it joy to fall in these trials and tribulations you will face. It is only a test of your faith to see if you can stand the test of time. Yes, it will be hard and painful. Yes, it will be uncomfortable but God will get the glory in the end. He just wants to see how far you can go with the pressure He will allow to be placed on your life. It is not easy, but it is worth it in the end. No test, no testimony.

**Discussion Questions:**

1. **When things seem to be spinning out of control how do you handle it?**

2. **Does everything go right for you, or is it just that you think there's no indication of anything ever going wrong?**

3. **Have you experienced anything in life where it turned your life upside down? How did you handle it, or did you ever get over it?**

4. **What does the statement, "No pain no gain," mean to you?**

**5. Do you feel like God allows you to go through situations for His glory? Why or why not?**

**Points to Discuss: After reading the lesson, go back and answer the questions in the lesson for an in-depth discussion.**

**Notes:**

## LESSON 3

# *A Walk of Faith, Part I*

**Foundation: Genesis 22:10-14**

*"And Abraham stretched forth his hand, and took the knife to slay his son. And the angel of the Lord called unto him out of heaven, and said, 'Abraham, Abraham,' and he said, 'Here am I.' And he said, 'Lay not thine hand upon the lad, neither do thou anything unto him; for now I know that thou fearest God, seeing thou hast not withheld thy son, thine only son from Me.' And Abraham lifted up his eyes, and looked, and behold behind him a ram caught in a thicket by his horns; and Abraham went and took the ram, and offered him up for a burnt offering in the stead of his son. And Abraham called the name of that place Jehovah-Jireh: as it is said to this day, 'In the mount of the Lord it shall be seen.'"*

### A. Confirming Your Faith

Abraham took his donkey, his son, and two of his young men, and clave the wood for the burnt offering; he arose and went to the place which God had told him. There, he was getting ready to offer his only son Isaac as a burnt offering unto God. God will order your steps if you just keep trusting and believing in Him. Just like Abraham, you will know that God shall supply all of your needs according to His riches in glory. Don't faint; just wait. Wait, I say, on the Lord. "For yet a little while, and He that shall come will come, and will not tarry" (Hebrews 10:37). "I will lift up mine eyes unto the hills, from whence cometh my help. My help cometh from the Lord, which made heaven and earth" (Psalm 121:1, 2). Can your faith be confirmed just as Abraham's was?

## B. Our Provider

Remember Shadrach, Meshach, and Abednego, the three boys in the fiery furnace: they knew that the God they served was more than enough. They refused to worship any pagan god. Their Provider was with them in the fiery furnace and caused all men to see and believe that our God is a true provider. He allowed them to come out of the high degree fire untouched, unscarred, and set free from the bondage and the troubles of another leader who was not our Jehovah-Jireh, "The Lord Will Provide." "Then Nebuchadnezzar the king was astonished, and rose up in haste, and spake and said unto his counselors, 'Did not we cast three men bound into the midst of the fire?' They answered and said unto the king, 'True, O king.' He answered and said, 'Lo, I see four men loose, walking in the midst of the fire, and they have no hurt; and the form of the fourth is like the Son of God.' Then Nebuchadnezzar came near to the mouth of the burning fiery furnace, and spake, and said, 'Shadrach, Meshach, and Abednego, ye servants of the most high God, come forth, and come hither.' Then Shadrach, Meshach, and Abednego, came forth of the midst of the fire. And the princes, governors, and captains, and the king's counselors, being gathered together, saw these men, upon whose bodies the fire had no power, nor was a hair of their head singed, neither were their coats changed, nor the smell of fire had passed on them. Then Nebuchadnezzar spake, and said, 'Blessed be the God of Shadrach, Meshach, and Abednego, who hath sent His angel, and delivered His servants that trusted in Him, and have changed the king's word, and yielded their bodies, that they might not serve nor worship any god, except their own God. Therefore, I make a decree, that every people, nation, and language, which speak anything amiss against the God of Shadrach, Meshach, and Abednego, shall be cut in pieces, and their houses shall be made a dunghill, because there is no other God that can deliver after this sort'" (Daniel 3:24-29).

It takes trials and tribulations on every hand for you to truly understand how God is good. He will not take you to it if He can't bring you through it. Our God is more than enough. He is our strong tower, our bright and morning star. He will deliver us from dangers seen and unseen, and from tragedies seen on every hand. Whatever your concerns may be, take it to God in prayer. Whatever trial, death call, anxiety, disbelief, concern, or whatever it may be, take it to God in prayer and leave it there. As indicated in 1 Peter 5:7, "Casting all your care upon him; for He careth for you." Whatever may be going wrong, whatever may be a big deal, whatever may be a need, want, or desire, seek God first and make it clearer than anything. He will give you the desires of your heart if you make it plain. He will turn your midnights into day. He will purify your heart and make it whiter than snow. Cry out like David. "Create in me a clean heart, O God; and renew a right spirit within me. Cast me not away from Thy presence; and take not Thy Holy Spirit from me. Restore unto me the joy of Thy salvation; and uphold me with Thy free spirit. Then will I teach transgressors Thy ways; and sinners shall be converted unto Thee" (Psalm 51:10-13).

### C. Fear Not!

"And all Judah rejoiced at the oath: for they had sworn with all their heart, and sought Him with their whole desire; and He was found of them; and the Lord gave them rest round about" (2 Chronicles 15:15). Just seek Jehovah-Jireh in times of trouble, when there is trouble on every hand. When people despitefully misuse you, do not care for you, and cannot seem to put you into their equation, shake the dust off of your feet and keep going because God has called you blessed, and He knows the circumstances and situations to which you will be exposed. Try God, and He will deliver you and work it out. God said, "Don't be afraid of their countenance; their facial expressions don't mean anything. Tell them what thus saith the Lord and I'll make your way straight and the road clearer for you to follow." "Be not afraid of their faces; for I am with Thee to deliver Thee,' saith the Lord. Then the Lord put forth His hand, and touched my mouth. And the Lord said unto me, 'Behold, I have put my words in thy mouth'" (Jeremiah 1:8, 9).

God does not want His children to be fearful of speaking and doing on His behalf. He indicated that He'd put the words in our mouths and give us wisdom beyond measure. Why do you fear people? As long as you are hearkening to the voice of the Lord, you will be fine. You must have a clear understanding and relationship with Him. God will grant you wisdom beyond measures to speak and perform on His behalf. When you think people are not listening, that's when they hear you loud and clearly. Speak the word from the Lord, and watch Him deliver His people back to Him. Do something good for someone else, and watch God bless it.

### D. Rise in Faith for Christ

Rise, and stand up for Christ. Even when everybody around you is wrong, still seek Christ, and take a full stand for Him. Even when your back is against the wall, stand for Christ. If you do not stand for something, you will fall for anything. Do not settle and compromise; stand for Christ, and watch Him deliver you. Watch Him turn your midnights into day. Watch Him make your stormy days sunny. Watch Him make a better day ahead for you after all. The road may seem rough, but your trials will not last always. "For His anger endureth but a moment; in His favor is life: weeping may endure for a night, but joy cometh in the morning" (Psalm 30:5). According to James, "My brethren, count it all joy when ye fall into divers temptations; knowing this, that the trying of your faith worketh patience. But let patience have her perfect work, that ye may be perfect and entire, wanting nothing. If any of you lack wisdom, let him ask of God, that giveth to all men liberally, and upbraideth not; and it shall be given him" (James 1:2-5). When you fall into various trails, just stand still and see the salvation of the Lord. He knows all about it, and He cares for you. When God sees your faith activated even in difficult times, He will respond to your every need. Just have faith!

**Discussion Questions:**

1. **Is God more than enough for you? Have you tried Him when times are frightening and life threatening? How was your experience?**

2. **Has there ever been a time when you thought God was not with you? Did He come through or not? Explain.**

3. **Do you believe God's timing is not your timing? Explain what that means to you and relate it to a situation in your life.**

4. **Have you ever had a situation where you wanted to confront someone about a situation but felt intimidated or unsupported? What did you do? What could you have done differently to make matters better?**

5. **Has there ever been a time when something bad happened over and over again and it didn't seem like it would ever end? How did you or how are you handling it?**

6. **Do you believe Christ will allow you to go through trying times and not be there for you? Why or why not?**

**Points to Discuss: After reading the lesson, go back and answer the questions in the lesson for an in-depth discussion.**

**Notes:**

## LESSON 4

# A Walk of Faith, Part II

**Foundation: Hebrews 11:6**

*"But without faith it is impossible to please Him; for he that cometh to God must believe that He is, and that He is a rewarder of them that diligently seek Him."*

### A. By Faith We Understand

Without faith, it is impossible to please God. "And Jesus said unto them, Because of your unbelief: for verily I say unto you, If ye have faith as a grain of mustard seed, ye shall say unto this mountain, "Remove hence to yonder place," and it shall remove; and nothing shall be impossible unto you. Howbeit this kind goeth not out but by prayer and fasting" (Matthew 17:20, 21). If your faith is greater in Christ, you will go where He leads you and follow His rules and commands. God is orchestrating His people to obedience. Remember, obedience is better than sacrifice. If you do not allow the Lord to use you, He will find someone else willing to be used. You must be willing to be an obedient, humble, and faithful servant of God. "Casting down imaginations, and every high thing that exalteth itself against the knowledge of God, and bringing into captivity every thought to the obedience of Christ. And having in a readiness to revenge all disobedience, when your obedience is fulfilled" (2 Corinthians 10:5, 6). If He tells you to go, tell Him to send you; "For I am your faithful servant, I will go." "Exhort servants to be obedient unto their own masters, and to please them well in all things; not answering again, not purloining, but showing all good fidelity that they may adorn the doctrine of God our Savior in all things" (Titus 2:9, 10). When trials fall on either side, just remain focused on God and know that it is a testing of your faith. To whom much is given, much is required. "But He that knew not, and did commit things worthy of stripes, shall be beaten with few stripes. For unto whomsoever much is given, of him shall be much required; and to whom men have committed much, of him they will ask the more" (Luke 12:48).

**B. Seek God's Instructions**

If He leads you to the wilderness, go and ask Him to meet you there. The Lord spoke to Joshua, the son of Nun, saying, "There shall not any man be able to stand before thee all the days of thy life; as I was with Moses, so I will be with thee. I will not fail thee, nor forsake thee" (Joshua 1:5). At a time like this, you need to be as gentle as a dove and as wise as a serpent. "Behold, I send you forth as sheep in the midst of wolves: be ye therefore wise as serpents, and harmless as doves" (Matthew 10:16). Keep your eyes and ears open at all times to seek instructions from God. "And now, Lord, behold their threatening: and grant unto Thy servants, that with all boldness they may speak Thy word, by stretching forth Thine hand to heal; and that signs and wonders may be done by the name of Thy holy Child, Jesus" (Acts 4:29, 30). We must keep in mind that humility, meekness, longsuffering, and joy are our portions. If we continue to lay prostrate, fasting and praying and seeking God, He will lead us to our divine place in His Kingdom. God is getting us ready to have dominion over the earth. "A good man leaveth an inheritance to his children's children; and the wealth of the sinner is laid up for the just" (Proverbs 13:22). The just are about to reap the benefits of God. If we would just take the time to focus on the many plans, strategies, and key points God has in store for us, and if we would just keep our minds stayed on Jesus, then we would see the promises of God. "He shall have dominion also from sea to sea and from the river unto the ends of the earth" (Psalm 72:8).

**C. Wait on the Lord**

We must have the faith of Abraham, Isaac, Moses, Jacob, Joseph, Enoch, and Noah. These were the many facets of God's glory in the kingdom. They all had faith in the promises of God. They did not let go until it came to pass. Their reward was greater because of their patience and longsuffering. "That ye be not slothful, but followers of them who through faith and patience inherit the promises" (Hebrews 6:12). It will come in due time. Wait on the Lord, and He shall renew your strength. Wait on the Lord, and He will give you guidance and better understanding. Wait on the Lord, and He will make your gloomy nights turn into victorious days. Wait, I say, on the Lord. Just wait. He will direct your path. Jesus will never leave you nor forsake you. "Wait on the Lord; be of good courage, and He shall strengthen thine heart. Wait, I say, on the Lord" (Psalm 27:14).

**Discussion Questions:**

1. **What is "mustard seed" faith, and how does it relate to you?**

2. **Do you believe God can do anything but fail? What proof do you have?**

3. **Do you truly seek instructions from God and adhere to His every command?**

4. **Do you desire to have a closer relationship in which you are able to hear more clearly from God? Do you believe it's possible?**

5. **Is it worth it to wait on the Lord? How do you know?**

**Points to Discuss: After reading the lesson, go back and answer the questions in the lesson for an in-depth discussion.**

**Notes:**

## LESSON 5

# *The Coming of the Lord*

**Foundation: Malachi 4:1-3**

*"'FOR, behold, the day cometh, that shall burn as an oven; and all the proud, yea, and all that do wickedly, shall be stubble; and the day that cometh shall burn them up, saith the Lord of hosts, that it shall leave them neither root nor branch. But unto you that fear My name shall the Son of Righteousness arise with healing in His wings; and ye shall go forth, and grow up as calves of the stall. And ye shall tread down the wicked; for they shall be as ashes under the soles of your feet in the day that I shall do this,' saith the Lord of hosts."*

### A. The Great Day of God

The day is coming when God is going to bring about a mighty change in His kingdom. All of His humble and faithful servants will be ready to go into the highways and byways telling people about Christ. He is making provisions for His vision. Sons and daughters are going to cry out for a change. There is going to be a shifting in the atmosphere where parents will want to assist with the many demands of God for their children. They will be seeking a change and different strategies to make life better for the upbringing of their children. If everybody will corporately fast and pray, things will change for the betterment of the kingdom. People are growing tired and weary of the existence of things on their jobs, in their homes, and in their schools. Prophet Elijah will come back and confess to the people the rightful stands they need to take in order for things to get better. "And Jesus answered and said unto them, 'Elijah truly shall first come, and restore all things. But I say unto you, That Elijah is come already, and they knew whatsoever they knew him not, but have done unto him whatsoever they listed. Likewise shall also the Son of man suffer of them" (Matthew 17:11, 12).

**B. What's Your Vision?**

Write the vision; make it plain for everyone to understand so people can run with it and make provision for it to come to pass. Where are the volunteers who are advocates for the children? Where are the sponsors and supporters for the youth in the community? Who is willing to take a stand and make it work so that the children can see how things are happening on their behalf? "I WILL stand upon my watch, and set me upon the tower, and will watch to see what He will say unto me, and what I shall answer when I am reproved. And the Lord answered me, and said, 'Write the vision, and make it plain upon tables, that he may run that readeth it. For the vision is yet for an appointed time, but at the end it shall speak, and not lie: though it tarry, wait for it; because it will surely come, it will not tarry. Behold, his soul which is lifted up is not upright in him, but the just shall live by his faith" (Habakkuk 2:1-4).

**C. Come Out of Hiding**

It is time for the "true Christians" to come forth and take a stand for Christ, leaning and depending on Him to carry it out. Fast and pray, seek His face, and ask for direction and leadership for things to come to pass. In order for things to work, everyone (all parents, sponsors, and supporters) must be on one accord seeking a different atmosphere that is not like the norm. Where are the true believers? Where are the laborers? Where are the ones looking for the shifting in the atmosphere? There shouldn't be any doubt or confusion. "And I set my face unto the Lord God, to seek by prayer and supplications, with fasting, and sackcloth, and ashes. And I prayed unto the Lord my God, and made my confession, and said, 'O Lord, the great and dreadful God, keeping the covenant and mercy to them that love Him, and to them that keep His commandments, we have sinned, and have committed iniquity, and have done wickedly, and have rebelled, even by departing from Thy precepts and from Thy judgments" (Daniel 9:3-5).

**Discussion Questions:**

1. **Do you have a vision burning inside of you, but you're afraid to go forward with it? Why are you afraid to step out on faith?**

2. **Do you believe God placed the vision in your heart to bring it to past?**

3. **When was the last time you fasted and prayed to hear from God? Did you get any results?**

4. **Do you believe God hears and answers prayers? Why or why not?**

5. **Has anything ever happened when you did not have faith in God and all hope was gone? Why did you give up? What did it cost you in the end?**

6. **If you could do something different about the vision/situation, what would you do?**

7. **Are you ready to come out of hiding for Christ and make a difference in your surrounding?**

**Points to Discuss: After reading the lesson, go back and answer the questions in the lesson for an in-depth discussion.**

**Notes:**

## LESSON 6

# The Journey Begins

**Foundation: 2 Samuel 9:2-13**

*"And there was of the house of Saul a servant whose name was Ziba. And when they had called him unto David, the king said unto him, 'Art thou Ziba!' And he said, 'Thy servant is he.' And the king said, 'Is there not yet any of the house of Saul, that I may shew the kindness of God unto him?' And Ziba said unto the king, 'Jonathan hath yet a son, which is lame on his feet.' And the king said unto him, 'Where is he?' And Ziba said unto the king, 'Behold, he is in the house of Machir the son of Ammiel, in Lo-debar.' Then King David sent, and fetched him out of the house of Machir, the son of Ammiel, from Lo-debar. Now when Mephibosheth, the son of Jonathan, the son of Saul, was come unto David, he fell on his face, and did reverence. And David said, 'Mephibosheth.' And he answered, 'Behold thy servant.' And David said unto him, 'Fear not; for I will surely show thee kindness for Jonathan thy father's sake, and will restore thee all the land of Saul thy father; and thou shalt eat bread at my table continually.'"*

### A. Life's Journey

Ziba was a servant of the house of Saul. King David asked him was there still someone of the house of Saul to whom He may show the kindness of God. There was still Jonathan's son, Mephibosheth, who was lame on his feet. Mephibosheth dwelt in Jerusalem eating continually at the king's table, as one of the king's sons. In the same way that Mephibosheth received David's kindness, God says, "I am storing up blessings for you–rich blessings beyond measure. There shall continually be dwelling places for your sons and daughters to dwell because they shall be called Blessed. Wherever your feet may tread, it shall be blessed. Whatever your soul desires, it shall be blessed. Stay away, and walk away, from negativity. Stay positive in all you do and say. Bring peace to chaotic situations and make sure all that is done is decent and in order." Make your request made known unto God, and He will restore all that the cankerworm has stolen from you. "And I will restore to you the years that the locust hath eaten, the cankerworm, and the caterpillar, and the palmerworm, my great army which I sent among you. And ye shall eat in plenty, and be satisfied, and praise the name of the Lord your God that hath dealt wondrously with you, and My people shall never be ashamed. And ye shall know that I am in the midst of Israel, and that I am the Lord your God and none else, and My people shall never be ashamed" (Joel 2:25-27). Mephibosheth was involved in what is called generational curses. Not only did he suffer being lame on his feet, but his father Jonathan was killed by King David. This caused him to be without in many aspects. Due to the Lord allowing favor on his life, he was able to be redeemed from generational curses by King David. Generational curses can be handed down from our ancestors who had issues, sin and other things that may affect us in our lives. We have a tendency to repeat the same bad habits as them. This goes through the life span of our descendants (our children and our children's children). It's best to seek Christ for a change immediately when you recognize doing the same things as your parents or other relatives who has had an impact on your life.

**B. Embark on the Journey of a Lifetime**

You are about to embark on a journey that may seem challenging, but it is worth the wait in every aspect. People are looking at you from a different perspective, and they are seeking your opinions and persuasions for things that you may say and respond to that will determine their destination in life. As you speak the word of the Lord, do not let disfigured faces intimidate you. Do and say as God authorizes so that you do not compromise with lowly brothers/sisters who are not going anywhere in life. "Don't stress, and don't fear because the earth is the Lord's and the fullness thereof. Ask anything that you desire, and I'll supply all of your needs according to My riches in glory," says the Lord. "Keep treading and staying fast in faith, and I will deliver you from all of your adversaries. Right now, you are being pruned to show Me what you are made of. Right now, you will be humiliated and disgraced for My name's sake because people are not accustomed to your boldness because of your quietness that you proclaim to have. Stop the nonsense, and speak the truth. You will be respected and appreciated more when they can see the realness in all you do and say. Speak everything in My name, and I will give you rest and peace that surpasses all understanding. And in all thy ways, acknowledge Me, and I shall direct your path," says the Lord of hosts. "But when the fullness of the time was come, God sent forth His Son, made of a woman, made under the law, to redeem them that were under the law, that we might receive the adoption of sons. And because ye are sons, God hath sent forth the Spirit of His Son into your hearts, crying, 'Abba, Father.' Wherefore, thou art no more a servant, but a son; and if a son, then an heir of God through Christ" (Galatians 4:4-7).

**C. Forgive**

"Take heed to yourselves: if thy brother trespass against thee, rebuke him, and if he repent, forgive him. And if he trespass against thee seven times in a day, and seven times in a day turn again to thee, saying, 'I repent,' thou shalt forgive him" (Luke 17:3, 4). It is your Christian duty not to take offense at what people say and do. Forgiveness is an act of submission to the Lord. We all submit to a spirit. It is our sole duty to forgive others and to treat them as we would have them treat us. Regardless of how other people make you feel, what they say, or whatever the circumstances may be, our job is to love one another. We cannot hold grudges, misunderstandings, or treachery to heart. The major task of where you are today is to live peaceably with everybody. "If it be possible, as much as lieth in you, live peaceably with all men. Dearly beloved, avenge not yourselves, but rather give place unto wrath: for it is written, VENGEANCE IS MINE; I WILL REPAY, saith the Lord" (Romans 12:18, 19). It does not matter if people "make you sick," or if you do not like the way people act. It is not your job to judge anyone; your main task is to get the job done and to do it well.

**D. Live**

In order to be a spiritual leader, you must lead by example. Be willing to stand up to others when they're wrong. At the same time, make sure you are doing and saying what is right. And in the midst of living righteously, remember that it is okay to enjoy life and not to be a stickler about everything. Live a little, and enjoy life for what it is worth. You will be glad that you did. Find things to laugh about and seek ways to enjoy the pleasures of life. Remember: God made this world for us to enjoy. According to John 10:10, Jesus died that we might have life and have it more abundantly. "How can I live if I am not comfortable? How can I play and enjoy others when somebody else is watching me? How can I enjoy the finer things in life when bills have to be paid?" These are questions sticklers and self-conscious people ask. The main thing you need to be concerned with is that you are doing the best you know how, and that everything will be fine.

## E. Do Not Allow Others to Judge You

If you increase your watching and listening techniques, then you will find that birds of a feather flock together. So what if people criticize you? Just because they are not walking in your shoes does not mean their judgment call matters. So what if they misuse and talk about you, saying that you never do anything right? Who are they to judge you? "JUDGE not, that ye be not judged. For with what judgment ye judge, ye shall be judged, and with what measure ye mete, it shall be measured to you again. And why beholdest thou the mote that is in thy brother's eye, but considerest not the beam that is in thine own eye? Or how wilt thou say to thy brother, 'Let me pull out the mote out of thine eye,' and, behold, a beam is in thine own eye? Thou hypocrite! First cast out the beam out of thine own eye, and then shalt see clearly to cast out the mote out of thy brother's eye" (Matthew 7:1-5). "Judge not, and ye shall not be judged; condemn not, and ye shall not be condemned; forgive, and ye shall be forgiven" (Luke 6:37). "A good man out of the good treasure of his heart bringeth forth that which is good; and an evil man out of the evil treasure of his heart bringeth forth that which is evil, for of the abundance of the heart his mouth speaketh" (Luke 6:45).

## F. Relate, Relax, and Release

If you do not seem to fit in, it is probably because you have not allowed yourself the opportunity to relate, relax, and release. Relate to other people and their many different ways. Just because they are doing something does not mean that you have to do it. Make personal judgment calls, and be yourself. It is okay not to blend, just be able to understand and respect others. This is what it means to relate. Relax around difficult people and situations. Sometimes it helps when everybody is not uptight and in an uproar about things. It is better to be in a humble and calm state than to be flustered and too concerned. "Let your moderation be known unto all men. The Lord is at hand. Be anxious for nothing, but in everything by prayer and supplication, with thanksgiving, let your requests be made known unto God. And the peace of God, which passeth all understanding, shall keep your hearts and minds through Christ Jesus" (Philippians 4:5-7).

Most people only care about themselves and their own situations. So who are you to talk? Chill out, and let nature have its way. Sometimes it works out better in the end to have little to say and let others burn themselves. It will all show up in the end. Release yourself from anxiety, depression, and fear. Once you get away from anxiety, you tend to feel better and look better. People are more apt to accept you when you release your feelings in a positive manner. When you are depressed, turn it over to Jesus, and He will work it out. If you are not sure if you are depressed or not, "pray without ceasing" (1 Thessalonians 5:17), and God will give you a breakthrough. When you fast and pray for yourself and others, the self-denial helps you to strengthen your spiritual being. "Moreover when ye fast, be not as the hypocrites, of a sad countenance, for they disfigure their faces that they may appear unto men to fast. Verily I say unto you, they have their reward. But thou, when thou fastest, anoint thine head, and wash thy face that thou appear not unto men to fast, but unto thy Father which is in secret. And thy Father, which seeth in secret, shall reward thee openly" (Matthew 6:16-18). "I WILL lift up mine eyes unto the hills, from whence cometh my help. My help cometh from the Lord, who made heaven and earth" (Psalm 121:1, 2).

**G. Fear God!**

"For God hath not given us the spirit of fear, but of power, and of love, and of a sound mind" (2 Timothy 1:7). Once we set aside time to fear God and to live a God-fearing lifestyle, then will the reward be greater in heaven. Do not fear people who are not living right but are constantly saying that they are, putting on a dog-and-pony show for others. God sees and knows all. They are only fooling themselves. "He that saith, 'I know Him,' and keepeth not His commandments, is a liar, and the truth is not in him. But he that hateth his brother is in darkness, and walketh in darkness, and knoweth not whither he goeth because that darkness hath blinded his eyes" (1 John 2:4, 11). "But I say unto you, love your enemies; bless them that curse you; do good to them that hate you, and pray for them which despitefully use you and persecute you" (Matthew 5:44). Once they have had a taste of their own medicine, they will begin to seek the true salvation of God and come back to apologize and admire you for being a firm believer of Christ. "Be not deceived; God is not mocked. For whatsoever a man soweth, that shall he also reap, for he that soweth to his flesh shall of the flesh reap corruption, but he that soweth to the Spirit shall of the Spirit reap life everlasting" (Galatians 6:7, 8). "Finally, my brethren, be strong in the Lord, and in the power of His might. Put on the whole armor of God, that ye may be able to stand against the wiles of the devil" (Ephesians 6:10, 11). Living a life that is fearful of Christ is freedom. In other words, when you fear God, you will not consciously sin because Jesus knew of no sins. You will constantly die to flesh daily so that your spirit man will be in charge of your actions and the words that you say. It is not an easy process, but once you put it into force, it will be easier to handle life. You must desire and willingly take a daily walk with God. Pray for directions and guidance and He will see you through. See Psalm 111:10 where it tells you that the beginning of wisdom is the fear of the Lord.

## H. Be an Acceptable Servant

When you have done all that you can do, still stand firm in the knowledge and belief of Christ. He will unveil Himself and shine as pure gold. Take the Christian stand, walk with God, and He will bring you out whiter than snow. "'Come now, and let us reason together,' saith the Lord. 'Though your sins be as scarlet, they shall be as white as snow; though they be red like crimson, they shall be as wool. If ye be willing and obedient, ye shall eat the good of the land" (Isaiah 1:18, 19). Get to know Him one-on-one, and He will make your midnights turn into day and make your smile as bright as the sunshine. Get on board the night train of God, and let Him turn your life around.

It's okay to live a pure, holy, and acceptable life for God. Even when the enemy tries to use his tricks and schemes, you should take a stand for what you believe in. Christ is forever seeking diligent workers who know Him one-on-one. When you establish a relationship with Christ, then you will know who you are and whose you are. "Yea, and all that will live godly in Christ Jesus shall suffer persecution. But evil men and seducers shall wax worse and worse, deceiving, and being deceived" (2 Timothy 3:12, 13). You do not have to second guess or try to fit in because it is alright when you do not. Just because people marvel at you when you come around, it does not necessarily mean they like or love you. Sometimes they do it because it is the only thing they know to do. Just be yourself, and let God do the rest. I say all of this in Jesus' name. Amen! "Marvel not, my brethren, if the world hates you" (1 John 3:13). "For the grace of God that bringeth salvation hath appeared to all men teaching us that denying ungodliness and worldly lusts, we should live soberly, righteously, and godly in this present world, looking for that blessed hope and the glorious appearing of the great God and our Savior Jesus Christ, who gave Himself for us, that He might redeem us from all iniquity, and purify unto Himself a peculiar people, zealous of good works. These things speak, and exhort and rebuke with all authority. Let no man despise thee" (Titus 2:11-15). "Let this mind be in you, which was also in Christ Jesus. Who, being in the form of God, thought it not robbery to be equal with God" (Philippians 2:5, 6).

**Discussion Questions:**

1. **Are you preparing blessings for your heritage?**

2. **Do you believe generational curses can be broken?**

3. **How are you making a difference to change generational curses in your family?**

4. **Have you experienced a change in friends/associates lately? Do you feel it was for your good or working against you?**

5. **Do you believe everything works for your good and in your favor?**

6. **Are you easy to take offense when someone insults you? What are the results? Is it worth it in the end?**

7. **Do you resolve issues with a fight or do you calmly get your point across?**

8. **Do you lead by example or do you believe in "do as I say and not as I do?" Is it a characteristic of God?**

9. **How are you living in abundance according to the Lord?**

**10. What are you speaking/saying to others out of the abundance of your heart? Are you positive or negative?**

**11. Will God be pleased with what you say and do? Is there room for improvement?**

**12. Are you quick to judge others? Why do you feel comfortable judging others? Does it make you feel better to find fault in others and not yourself?**

**13. Do you know how to relax, relate, and release to others and make them feel better or relaxed enough around you? If you're always uptight, check yourself.**

**14. Why is it important to fear God?**

**15. Do you believe people need people? Why or Why not?**

**16. Do you have a mind like Christ to do and say that which is pleasing in His sight? Will he get the glory through you?**

**Points to Discuss: After reading the lesson, go back and answer the questions in the lesson for an in-depth discussion.**

**Notes:**

# LESSON 7

# *Seeking God for Healing and Spiritual Power*

**Foundation: Luke 7:1-17**

*"NOW when He had ended all His sayings in the audience of the people, He entered into Capernaum. And a certain centurion's servant, who was dear unto him, was sick and ready to die. And when he heard of Jesus, he sent unto Him the elders of the Jews, beseeching Him that He would come and heal His servant. And when they came to Jesus, they besought Him instantly, saying, that he was worthy for whom He should do this. 'For he loveth our nation, and he hath built us a synagogue.' Then Jesus went with them. And when He was now not far from the house, the centurion sent friends to Him, saying unto Him, 'Lord, trouble not Thyself, for I am not worthy that Thou shouldest enter under my roof. Wherefore, neither thought I myself worthy to come unto Thee, but say in a word, and my servant shall be healed. For I also am a man set under authority, having under me soldiers, and I say unto one, 'Go,' and he goeth, and to another, 'Come,' and he cometh; and to my servant, 'Do this,' and he doeth it.' When Jesus heard these things, He marveled at him, and turned him about, and said unto the people that followed Him, 'I say unto you, I have not found so great faith, no, not in Israel.' And they that were sent, returning to the house, found the servant whole that had been sick. And it came to pass the day after, that He went into a city called Nain, and many of His disciples went with Him and much people. Now when He came nigh to the gate of the city, behold, there was a dead man carried out, the only son of his mother, and she was a widow, and much people of the city was with*

*her. And when the Lord saw her, He had compassion on her, and said unto her, 'Weep not.' And He came and touched the bier, and they that bore him stood still, and He said, 'Young man, I say unto thee, arise.' And he that was dead sat up and began to speak. And He delivered him to his mother."*

### A. Mustard Seed Faith

If you have faith the size of a mustard seed, you can tell a mountain to move, and it must obey. If your faith exceeds the norm, you can have anything you want in Jesus' name. If you live according to the word and have the word instilled in you, you can have all that God ordains for your life. If you would just put aside the earthly man and pick up the spiritual man, you will begin to see the plans God has for your life. "If we live in the Spirit, let us also walk in the Spirit. Let us not be desirous of vain glory, provoking one another, envying one another" (Galatians 5:25, 26).

### B. Seek God

If you set aside time for God on a daily basis and seek His face, He will come and sup with you and give you wisdom beyond measures that will prove His final word. "If My people, which are called by My name, shall humble themselves, and pray, and seek My face, and turn from their wicked ways, then will I hear from heaven, and will forgive their sin, and will heal their land" (2 Chronicles 7:14). The earth is the Lord's and the fullness thereof, so why are you worried? Why do you allow people and things to get the best of you? "Seek ye the Lord while He may be found, call ye upon Him while He is near" (Isaiah 55:6). If you would seek the Lord and worship Him in spirit and in truth, you will find the greater reward He has for you. "God is a Spirit, and they that worship Him must worship Him in spirit and in truth" (John 4:24). No man can see the face of the Lord and live, but all men can seek His salvation and have a reward to live for Him and through Him. "The Lord is good unto them that wait for Him, to the soul that seeketh Him. It is good that a man should both hope and quietly wait for the salvation of the Lord" (Lamentations 3:25, 26). Greater is he that is in the Lord than he that is in the world. "Ye are of God, little children, and have overcome them because greater is He that is in you, than he that is in the world" (1 John 4:4). Do you realize that God died and left His power here on earth so that you could do the same thing He was doing while He was here? You can have the power to heal the sick, raise the dead, and give sight to the blind. "But ye shall receive power, after that the Holy Ghost is come upon you. And ye shall be witnesses unto Me both in Jerusalem, and in all Judea, and in Samaria, and unto the uttermost part of the earth" (Acts 1:8).

What are you waiting for to make it happen? Who are you waiting on? Have you tested your faith? Are you living as God has called for your life? Do you know and see the just reward for your life? Are you seeking and giving God your full potential, or have you allowed man to get the best of you? Have you learned to settle for less and suffer for nothing? Have you not seen and have you not heard the things that have entered into the kingdom of God? God wants us to live by faith and not by sight. He wants our spiritual man to have all of the elements that He has allowed for our lives. If we would just set aside our outer beings and pull up our inner beings, then we will know what God has for our lives. We must learn to be spiritually-minded and not carnal. We must learn that discernment is a gift from God, if we only believe. "But the natural man receiveth not the things of the Spirit of God; for they are foolishness unto him. Neither can he know them, because they are spiritually discerned" (1 Corinthians 2:14). We must all put on the whole armor of God and watch Satan tremble and flee. He cannot do anything without first getting permission from God.

### C. Spiritual Empowerment

You have the power to be activated according to the Spirit. You have the power to love and enjoy life in its fullest. You have the power to tell the devil to flee from you, and he has to obey. You have the power to seek God for your eyes to see the greater reward above. When will you activate this right? When will you give God your fullest potential to be used by His Spirit? When will you put off the old man and seek God for righteousness and purity? Are you ready to live strictly for God? Are you ready to be spiritually-minded and know the plans God has for you? Are you ready to receive the full salvation from God? Be ye ready at all times. "But of that day and hour knoweth no man, no, not the angels of heaven, but My Father only" (Matthew 24:36). Will you be ready? Have you activated your true powers from God? Have they been tried, tested, and approved according to His word? Study the word, fast and pray, and God will make it plain and simple. It'll be just like a roadmap. Give your all to God. "Study to show thyself approved unto God, a workman that needeth not to be ashamed, rightly dividing the word of truth" (2 Timothy 3:15).

**Discussion Questions:**

1. **Do you believe God has a plan for your life?**

2. **Are you walking in the directions of the Lord?**

3. **Have you activated your spiritual man to obtain the favor of the Lord?**

4. **Have you received all of the blessings God has for you? Why or Why not?**

5. **Do you believe in functioning in the grace of God?**

6. **Is God your all in everything you do? If not, why won't you allow Him to use you?**

7. **Are you ready to allow God to use you as His vessel?**

8. **Are you ready to switch from the mundane way of doing things and start doing it from a spiritual perspective?**

**Points to Discuss: After reading the lesson, go back and answer the questions in the lesson for an in-depth discussion.**

**Notes:**

## LESSON 8

# *Let Go; Let God*

**Foundation: Acts 9:10-22**

*"And Saul arose from the earth; and when his eyes were opened, he saw no man: but they led him by the hand, and brought him into Damascus. And he was three days without sight, and neither did eat nor drink. And there was a certain disciple at Damascus, named Ananias; and to him said the Lord in a vision, 'Ananias.' And he said, 'Behold, I am here, Lord.' And the Lord said unto him, 'Arise, and go into the street which is called Straight, and inquire in the house of Judas for one called Saul of Tarsus: for, behold, he prayeth, and hath seen in a vision a man named Ananias coming in and putting his hand on him, that he might receive his sight.' Then Ananias answered, 'Lord, I have heard by many of this man, how much evil he hath done to Thy saints at Jerusalem. And here he hath authority from the chief priests to bind all that call on Thy name.' But the Lord said unto him, 'Go thy way; for he is a chosen vessel unto Me, to bear My name before the Gentiles, and kings, and the children of Israel. For I will show him how great things he must suffer for My name's sake'" (Acts 9:8-16).*

### A. Surrender and Peace

In doing evil, sometimes God will allow you to think that you are getting over for a while just to make you suffer for His name's sake. Saul persecuted and killed people who were following Christ. As he was on his way to Damascus, God stopped him in his tracks to turn his life around. Saul thought he was going to kill others who were following Christ, but God had a master plan for his life. Saul became Paul, and he became an ultimate follower of Christ. Just like God did it to Paul, he can surely do it to others. There are people in this world who do not realize how good they have it until it is all gone; afterwards, they realize that it was not that good after all. Many problems, situations, and circumstances all have a boundary through Jesus Christ because He is the author and finisher of our faith. "Looking unto Jesus, the author and finisher of our faith, who for the joy that was set before Him, endured the cross, despising the shame, and is set down at the right hand of the throne of God" (Hebrews 12:2). Once we look at the big picture in life, then are we all the more able to see the sacrifices and hardships that God allows us to experience. Everything happens for a reason and in due season. "And let us not be weary in well doing; for in due season we shall reap, if we faint not" (Galatians 6:9).

## B. Surrender to God

When you are chosen by God, He will allow your faith to be tested and tried all for His glory. You know some people may look at your life and assume that everything is wonderful and that you've got it all together, but you are sinning, living in lust, hate, envy, strife, and filth. It is at these times that God will allow all of your good things to come to an end because you have laid it all on the line for selfish reasons. Sin may not have an immediate effect on your life, but it is sure to come. Sometimes you'll see the effects of your sins in the lives of your offspring or through someone who is close to you. When you sin, you don't get to choose who suffers from the consequences. When God places His hands on your life, there is nothing you can do but surrender and get it together to live holy and acceptable for Him. "I beseech you therefore, brethren, by the mercies of God, that ye present your bodies a living sacrifice, holy, acceptable unto God, which is your reasonable service. And be not conformed to this world, but be ye transformed by the renewing of your mind, that ye may prove what is that good and acceptable, and perfect, will of God" (Romans 12: 1, 2). Not only will it help, but it blesses others who will see you because they knew you when you were in a mess in the world, but when you start living for Christ, all things are turned around and made much better for your life. God will reveal His ultimate plan for your life so that He can prove himself while living in and through you. People may be going through fiery trials, but once they come into contact with you and hear your life experiences and testimony, it will allow them to rejoice in the Lord as their souls are recovered and revived through you. Allow the Lord to come into your life and to use you as His vessel. "I returned, and saw under the sun, that the race is not to the swift, nor the battle to the strong, neither yet bread to the wise, nor yet riches to men of understanding, nor yet favor to men of skill; but time and chance happeneth to them all" (Ecclesiastes 9:11). Put up the good fight, and live a life that's worthy to be praised in Christ. He's our Lord and Savior and because of Him, we have life, and He will allow us to have it more abundantly.

**C. The Good Fight of Faith**

He will allow trials and tribulations to come into your life only to make you stronger in His faith. Once you have put up the good fight and have finished the race, then will you know that hope is there to lead and guide you through it all. Rest assured that everything is well through Christ that strengthens us. Live for God, and He will reveal His plan for your life. "For I through the law am dead to the law, that I might live unto God. I am crucified with Christ: nevertheless I live; yet not I, but Christ liveth in me; and the life which I now live in the flesh I live by the faith of the Son of God, who loved me, and gave Himself for me," (Galatians 2:19, 20). He will give you a vision that must be conquered through His name. Live a life that is free from sin, and watch God do the rest. He who gives a vision will surely make provisions in order for it to come to pass. Be blessed in the name of the Lord.

**D. Pursue Peace With All People**

"Wherefore lift up the hands which hang down, and the feeble knees; and make straight paths for your feet, lest that which is lame be turned out of the way; but let it rather be healed. Follow peace with all men, and holiness, without which no man shall see the Lord. Looking diligently lest any man fail of the grace of God; lest any root of bitterness springing up trouble you, and thereby many be defiled; Lest there be any fornicator, or profane person, as Esau, who for one morsel of meat sold his birthright. For ye know how that afterward, when he would have inherited the blessing, he was rejected: for he found no place of repentance, though he sought it carefully with tears" (Hebrews 12:12-17).

Seek the Lord first, and do good. There may be situations and circumstances that may cause you to want to give up, but you must stay strong and under the leadership and wisdom of God. Seek to do good, not looking for a pat on the back from men, but knowing that God is the author and finisher of your faith. Start with your family, seeking a difference for the better in them. You cannot change people, but you can change the way you think and see things. Put on the whole armor of God, and do that which is spoken from Him, and He shall direct your path. Do good and not evil. "In all thy ways acknowledge Him, and He shall direct thy paths. Be not wise in thine own eyes; fear the Lord, and depart from evil" (Proverbs 3:6, 7). Pray for all people. Do what you can for those who are with you and let the Lord lead the way. "Trust in the Lord with all thine heart; and lean not unto thine own understanding" (Proverbs 3:5). In all things, acknowledge Him, and He shall direct your path and mind. Keep your mind stayed on Jesus. "Thou wilt keep him in perfect peace, whose mind is stayed on Thee; because He trusteth in Thee. Trust ye in the Lord forever; for in the Lord Jehovah is everlasting strength" (Isaiah 26:3, 4). Speak to those who are fearful hearted. Be strong, do not fear. Speak what is right, but with salt. Let your thoughts be that of a sweet aroma–savory and pure. Do not let your left hand know what your right hand is doing. Be mindful of others. Treat them just like you want to be treated. Seek peace, and do good one to another. "Depart from evil, and do good; seek peace, and pursue it" (Psalm 34:14).

**Discussion Questions:**

1. **Have you suffered after you've done something or someone wrong?**

2. **Have past experiences come back to haunt you? If so, how? If not, do you believe it was the mercy of God?**

3. **Are you a selfish person? Has this caused problems in your relationship with others? Explain.**

4. **Has God given you a vision to fulfill, and you're still not responding? If so, what are you waiting for?**

5. **Do you make excuses for not reacting and responding to life situations and circumstances? Why or why not?**

**6. What does it mean not to let your left hand know what your right hand is doing?**

**Points to Discuss: After reading the lesson, go back and answer the questions in the lesson for an in-depth discussion.**

**Notes:**

## LESSON 9

# *Stay the Course*

**Foundation: Matthew 16:5-12**

*"And when His disciples were come to the other side, they had forgotten to take bread. Then Jesus said unto them, 'Take heed and beware of the leaven of the Pharisees and of the Sadducees'. And they reasoned among themselves, saying, 'It is because we have taken no bread,' which when Jesus perceived, He said unto them, 'O ye of little faith, why reason ye among yourselves, because ye have brought no bread? Do ye not yet understand, neither remember the five loaves of the five thousand, and how many baskets ye took up? Neither the seven loaves of the four thousand, and how many baskets ye took up? How is it that ye do not understand that I spake it not to you concerning bread, that ye should beware of the leaven of the Pharisees and of the Sadducees?' Then understood they how that He bade them not beware of the leaven of bread, but of the doctrine of the Pharisees and of the Sadducees."*

### A. Beware of the False Doctrines

Beware of people who try to get you to live and act according to their lifestyles, teaching, and preaching when what they say or do is not specified by the Word of God. There are times when others may teach their traditions as "gospel truth," but the Word of God does not support them. Also, there are situations where people are more apt to ridicule each other than support one another. We, as Christians, are to keep in mind our words and actions that are shown. We need to clean up our own ways and act according to the Gospel of Jesus Christ.

## B. God's Guidance

Once we have spoken true words of wisdom, we must be careful only to utter the things Christ would have us to say because this generation of people is untruthful, dishonest, wicked and do not like facing the truth. Our job is to stay before the Lord and allow Him to use us like He has never used us before. Don't be a fake follower of Christ who talks to others about what they should and should not be doing while you are living a life filled with sin. God is not pleased with this type of lifestyle. Be aware of people who are similar to this. They are false workers of Christ. Speak into their lives about truth and deliverance, for God is a spirit. We must worship Him in spirit and in truth. Speak deliverance into the very lives of those you encounter. Bring light into their lives by the way you live. It's okay to let them know that their lives are corrupt and outside of the will of God.

Pray these words of wisdom into their lives: "Although our situations and personal lives may be dim, our reactions are determined by our state of mind with Christ. Open the door and allow the Lord to come in your life. Allow Him to guide your thought processes and decisions. Once you open up and decide to follow Christ, He will never leave you nor forsake you, but He will give you a clearer direction and drive to follow Him even closer than before. Welcome His territory into your heart and allow Him to direct your path. There are things that may be uttered or spoken that will change lives forever. Your only hope and desire should be to wait on the Lord and be of good courage. Speak words of truth as you follow Christ for real. Don't live and speak false doctrines but stay the course for Christ in Jesus' name".

The enemy is waiting to destroy, but your job is to stay close to the Lord and to let Him direct your path and direction. Keep your eyes stayed on Christ, and watch His evolution of Love overflow in and through you. Be blessed in the name of the Lord. Do not let anything separate you from the Love of God, not death, principality, wickedness, envy, strife, nothing. "Who shall separate us from the love of Christ? Shall tribulation, or distress, or persecution, or famine, or nakedness, or peril, or sword" (Romans 8:35)? Seek the Lord, and do well. Try to live peaceably with all men. God loves you and He will never allow more to be put on you than you can bear. Become equipped and ready to do His will in your life. Wait, I say, on the Lord! He wants to be your Shepherd – to lead and guide you through everyday life situations and circumstances.

## C. Stay the Course

"But, beloved, we are persuaded better things of you, and things that accompany salvation, though we thus speak. For God is not unrighteous to forget your work and labor of love, which ye have showed toward His name, in that ye have ministered to the saints, and do minister. And we desire that every one of you do show the same diligence to the full assurance of hope unto the end; that ye be not slothful, but followers of them who through faith and patience inherit the promises. For when God made promise to Abraham, because He could swear by no greater, He sware by Himself, saying, SURELY BLESSING I WILL BLESS THEE, AND MULTIPLYING I WILL MULTIPLY THEE. And so, after he had patiently endured, he obtained the promise. For men verily swear by the greater: and an oath for confirmation is to them an end of all strife. Wherein God, willing more abundantly to show unto the heirs of promise the immutability of His counsel, confirmed it by an oath; that by two immutable things, in which it was impossible for God to lie, we might have a strong consolation, who have fled for refuge to lay hold upon the hope set before us, which hope we have as an anchor of the soul, both sure and steadfast, and which entereth into that within the veil. Whither the forerunner is for us entered, even Jesus, made a high priest for ever after the order of Melchizedek" (Hebrews 6:9-20).

God shows justice for those who love Him and endure until the end. "Though He slay me, yet will I trust in Him, but I will maintain mine own ways before Him" (Job 13:15). Oftentimes, people will be quick to judge you because of how <u>men</u> see you. That is why you have to put on the whole armor of God and stand against the wiles of the enemy. Once people see you for who you are, they will see Christ in you. "And Moses said unto the people, 'Fear ye not, stand still, and see the salvation of the Lord, which He will show to you today" (Exodus 14:13). Stand still, and let the Lord fight your battles. "The earth is the Lord's, and the fullness thereof; the world, and they that dwell therein" (Psalm 24:1). "Ye ask, and receive not, because ye ask amiss, that ye may consume it upon your lusts" (James 4:3). Start calling out the things you want and need from the Lord. "But my God shall supply all of your need according to His riches in glory by Christ Jesus" (Philippians 4:19).

Do not be weary, and do not faint, but just hold on to God's unchanging hand; He will grant you wisdom and peace. "The Lord said unto my Lord, 'Sit Thou at My right hand, until I make Thine enemies Thy footstool'. The Lord shall send the rod of Thy strength out of Zion: rule thou in the midst of Thine enemies. Thy people shall be willing in the day of Thy power, in the beauties of holiness from the womb of the morning: Thou hast the dew of Thy youth. The Lord hath sworn, and will not repent, Thou art a priest forever after the order of Melchizedek. The Lord at their right hand shall strike through kings in the day of

His wrath. He shall judge among the heathen, He shall fill the places with the dead bodies; He shall wound the heads over many countries. He shall drink of the brook in the way: therefore shall He lift up the head" (Psalm 110:1-7).

"PRAISE ye the Lord. I will praise the Lord with my whole heart, in the assembly of the upright, and in the congregation. The works of the Lord are great, sought out of all them that have pleasure therein. His work is honorable and glorious: and His righteousness endureth forever. He hath made His wonderful works to be remembered; the Lord is gracious and full of compassion. He hath given meat unto them that fear Him. He will ever be mindful of His covenant. He hath showed His people the power of His works, that He may give them the heritage of the heathen. The works of His hands are verity and judgment; all His commandments are sure. They stand fast forever and ever, and are done in truth and uprightness. He sent redemption unto His people: He hath commanded His covenant forever: holy and reverent is His name. The fear of the Lord is the beginning of wisdom; a good understanding have all they that do His commandments: His praise endureth forever" (Psalm 111:1-10).

**D. Ignore the Naysayers**

People feel and fear that you have more than what you actually need. Everybody is not happy for you, but you must stay the course and wait diligently on the Lord. Once you give your all to Jesus, He will give you strength and show grace and mercy towards you. No man can enter the Kingdom but by Jesus. Find Him, secure Him, establish a closer relationship with Him, and see His powers and blessing unveil before you.

Do not worry about what men say and do, just put on the breastplate of righteousness and the shield of faith. Let nothing separate you from the Love of God. Always keep the faith and stay the course and see God reveal Himself through you. Pray, pray and pray! You will see God come in and overshadow the enemy. Keep the faith, believe, and receive that which is already before you. Blessed is he who enters through the gate of righteousness than he who sits and leans toward men. "When the time comes for you to receive and do My will, you will know," says the Lord. Stay faithful, and stand the test. Do not say anything evil or wrong about anyone; just seek Christ in all things, and God will direct your path. He will lead and guide you through all of your trials, tribulations, and overcoming of joy. He will give you peace and rest in your times of dispute.

## E. Wait on the Lord

Wait on the Lord, and be of good courage. Wait on the Lord, and see Him manifest His Love to you. Man has no heaven or hell for anyone. His job is to encourage, to wait, and to pray. The Lord says, "When they condemn you for My name's sake, you should rejoice and know that I am God." Do not waiver, and do not worry. Just stay in touch, continue to pray, and seek God for words, guidance, and direction. Know that He is God and say, "I can do all things through Christ which strengthens me" (Philippians 4:13). Remember that man is on the defense and wants to see who can out do the other, but God says, "For His anger endureth but a moment; in His favor is life: weeping may endure for a night, but joy cometh in the morning" (Psalm 30:5).

Where is your faith? Do not waiver, and do not be in dismay. Let God fight your battles and let Him shine in and through you. "Behold, His soul which is lifted up is not upright in him: but the just shall live by his faith" (Habakkuk 2:4). Live as if it may end tomorrow. Enjoy life, and take in the goodness of God through Christ Jesus, our Lord and Savior.

## F. Forgiveness

Forgiveness is an inevitable part of life. People struggle with this area daily because they are constantly fighting in their flesh about why someone wronged them. Instead of just confessing to Christ their hang ups with others and their personal problems they put it off on others to make it seem as if it's the other person's problem. We as a generation have forgotten about "Charity." God said the greatest gift is "Love." When we start to love one another as Christ loves us then will we be better at forgiving others. It's not so much the situation than it is pride. We feel weak, relentless, and cowardly when we're forgiving others. What happened to turning the other cheek when someone slaps you? We must have a heart of forgiveness in order to see and believe the things Christ has for us. God said if we don't forgive others of their trespasses He won't forgive us of ours. If you're forgiven for yours, what's the outcome? It's time to wake up and to become meek and mild in forgiving others. Live the life of a champion for Christ in this area, and watch Him blossom through you. You should return evil with good. Didn't Jesus himself forgive others while He was on the cross?

Forgive people who owe you a debt; allow them to repay. Do not throw them into jail, and drag them in the courts. Instead, forgive their trespasses so that your heavenly Father forgives you. When someone owes you, rather see to it that God guards your heart and gives you a heart of forgiveness. Do unto others as you would have them do unto you. Even if they used you for your resources, forgive them. Watch what you say and how you say it. Do not be one with a mouth that goes on and on about somebody else's blessings and/or dysfunctions when you are torn down. Be mindful of others' feelings and thoughts. When people falsely accuse you or just do not like you because you are you, just allow God to protect you and continue being a child of the Most High. Do not be burnt with their ill temper and feelings and allow those spirits to transfer to you. Guard your heart, eyes, ears, and mouth. When the Spirit is functioning to fight your battles, you will know and understand that you do not have to entertain the devil. Do not fight fire with fire and ugly words; fight with truth from the heart. Pray for that brother or sister, and see God's salvation come into existence. When you die to the flesh, the spirit man will come to the forefront and handle uncomfortable situations.

"Then came Peter to Him, and said, 'Lord, how oft shall my brother sin against me, and I forgive him? Till seven times?' Jesus saith unto him, 'I say not unto thee, until seven times; but, until seventy times seven. Therefore is the kingdom of heaven likened unto a certain king, which would take account of his servants. And when he had begun to reckon, one was brought unto him, which owed him ten thousand talents. But forasmuch as he had not to pay, his lord commanded him to be sold, and his wife, and children, and all that he had, and payment to be made. The servant therefore fell down, and worshiped him, saying, "Lord, have patience with me, and I will pay thee all." Then the lord of that servant was moved with compassion, and loosed him, and forgave him the debt. But the same servant went out, and found one of his fellow servants, which owed him a hundred pence: and he laid hands on him, and took him by the throat, saying, "Pay me that thou owest." And his fellow servant fell down at his feet, and besought him, saying, "Have patience with me, and I will pay thee all." And he would not, but went and cast him into prison, till he should pay the debt. So when his fellow servants saw what was done, they were very sorry, and came and told unto their lord all that was done. Then his lord, after that he had called him, said unto him, "O thou wicked servant, I forgave thee all that debt, because thou desiredst me: Shouldest not thou also have had compassion on thy fellow servant, even as I had pity on thee? And his lord was wroth, and delivered him to the tormentors, till he should pay all that was due unto him. So likewise shall my heavenly Father do also unto you, if ye from your hearts forgive not everyone his brother their trespasses" (Matthew 18:21-35).

**Discussion Questions:**

1. **Have you encountered individuals who say one thing but do another?**

2. **How do you, or would you, handle people in a Christ-like way, who practice falsehood for Christ?**

3. **Are you a true follower of Christ, or do you fall sometimes?**

4. **Do you fall prey to temptation? Why or why not?**

5. **Do you share with others the things you need and want God to fulfill in your life? Why or why not?**

6. **Why is it so hard to forgive others?**

7. **Do you turn the other cheek when someone has wronged you? What do you do?**

8. **If Jesus can forgive others while He's redeeming His life for us, why can't we do the same for others?**

9. **Is it your desire to be like Christ? Explain.**

**10. Do you believe in the transfer of spirits? Why or why not?**

**Points to Discuss: After reading the lesson, go back and answer the questions in the lesson for an in-depth discussion.**

**Notes:**

# LESSON 10

# *Resting in the Lord*

**Foundation: Hebrews 3:15**

*"While it is said, TODAY IF YE WILL HEAR His VOICE, HARDEN NOT YOUR HEARTS, AS IN THE PROVOCATION."*

## A. Wanderers and the Promise of Rest (Unbelief)

He promised us that He will give us rest. He gives peace that surpasses all understanding. Once our minds are stayed on Jesus, then will we know our thoughts and mental capacity for His strength in our lives. May God grant us the things that He has solemnly placed before us and may He give us perfect peace in the times of a storm. Who does Jesus see you as? Allow Him to come in and put grace in your life. Do you understand that grace does not give you an excuse to sin? Grace gives you the power to walk away from sin. He'll grant rest to you because it will teach you to say no to ungodly activities and worldly desires. The Holy Spirit will give you the power to work out your own salvation with fear and trembling. It will also allow you to rest in the grace of God. "Moreover the law entered, that the offense might abound. But where sin abounded, grace did much more abound: that as sin hath reigned unto death, even so might grace reign through righteousness unto eternal life by Jesus Christ our Lord" (Romans 5:20, 21).

Jesus died so we can rest away from sin. We should rule and reign over sin. As Christians, we should expose sin for what it's worth. Sin shouldn't overpower us when we're in a struggle with it. We must learn to pray and seek the rest of God. There's hope for everyone who seeks freedom from sin. God can see the inner man; therefore, He knows our thoughts and can discern what we are planning to do carnally. Why fight a never ending battle? Die daily to the flesh and allow the spirit man to be activated. He knows the desires of your heart, whether or not they are carnal or spiritual. Remember, because we are in the likeness of Christ, we should know of no sin because He was tempted like us, yet without sin.

**B. Confidence in Christ**

"For we are made partakers of Christ, if we hold the beginning of our confidence steadfast unto the end, while it is said, TODAY IF YE WILL HEAR His VOICE, HARDEN NOT YOUR HEARTS AS IN THE PROVOCATION. For some, when they had heard, did provoke: howbeit not all that came out of Egypt by Moses. But with whom was He grieved forty years? Was it not with them that had sinned, whose carcasses fell in the wilderness? And to whom sware He that they should not enter into His rest, but to them that believed not? So we see that they could not enter in because of unbelief. LET us therefore fear, lest, a promise being left us of entering into His rest, any of you should seem to come short of it. For unto us was the gospel preached, as well as unto them: but the word preached did not profit them, not being mixed with faith in them that heard it. For we which have believed do enter into rest, as He said, As I HAVE SWORN IN MY WRATH, IF THEY SHALL ENTER INTO MY REST: although the works were finished from the foundation of the world. For He spake in a certain place of the seventh day on this wise, AND GOD DID REST THE SEVENTH DAY FROM ALL His WORKS. And in this place again, IF THEY SHALL ENTER INTO MY REST. Seeing therefore it remaineth that some must enter therein, and they to whom it was first preached entered not in because of unbelief. Again, He limiteth a certain day, saying in David, TODAY, and after so long a time; as it is said, TODAY IF YE WILL HEAR His VOICE, HARDEN NOT YOUR HEARTS. For if Jesus had given them rest, then would He not afterward have spoken of another day. There remaineth therefore a rest to the people of God. For He that is entered into His rest, He also hath ceased from His own works, as God did from his. Let us labor therefore to enter into that rest, lest any man fall after the same example of unbelief. For the word of God is quick, and powerful, and sharper than any two edged sword, piercing even to the dividing asunder of soul and spirit, and of the joints and marrow, and is a discerner of the thoughts and intents of the heart. Neither is there any creature that is not manifest in His sight: but all things are naked and opened unto the eyes of Him with whom we have to do. Seeing then that we have a great high priest, that is passed into the heavens, Jesus the Son of God, let us hold fast our profession. For we have not a high priest which cannot be touched with the feeling of our infirmities; but was in all points tempted like as we are, yet without sin. Let us therefore come boldly unto the throne of grace that we may obtain mercy, and find grace to help in time of need" (Hebrews 3:14-19: 4:1-16).

## C. Allow God to Lead and to Guide You

Hear what the Lord has to say; open your ears and eyes to His righteousness. If you hold fast to the promise, to the belief, and to the will of God, He will direct your path and make your narrow way straight and the light of the world brighter for you to see. There are circumstances and situations that may seem dim, but you must put on the whole armor of God and be guided by His promise and thought process. Seek the Lord first in all that you do; acknowledge His ways, and let Him lead and guide you into the path of righteousness for His name's sake. There are situations and circumstances that may not seem right to you, but you can't allow yourself to get all worked up about it. You must learn to lean and depend on the Lord for the right things to say and do. Some situations may seem bleak to the carnal eye and mind, but if you will wait on the Lord, He shall carry you through. No situation is too hard for God. He wants to come and see about you, but you must hold on, keep the faith, and know that He will make everything alright. Nothing, absolutely nothing, is too hard for God. Find your resting place in the bosom of God's heart, and know that He will never leave you nor forsake you. "And we know that all things work together for good to them that love God, to them who are the called according to His purpose" (Romans 8:28).

"Wherefore as the Holy Ghost saith, TODAY IF YE WILL HEAR His VOICE, HARDEN NOT YOUR HEARTS, AS IN THE PROVOCATION, IN THE DAY OF TEMPTATION IN THE WILDERNESS: WHEN YOUR FATHERS TEMPTED ME, PROVED ME, AND SAW MY WORKS FORTY YEARS. WHEREFORE I WAS GRIEVED WITH THAT GENERATION, AND SAID, THEY DO ALWAYS ERR IN THEIR HEART; AND THEY HAVE NOT KNOWN MY WAYS. SO I SWARE IN MY WRATH, THEY SHALL NOT ENTER INTO MY REST. Take heed, brethren, lest there be in any of you an evil heart of unbelief, in departing from the living God. But exhort one another daily, while it is called TODAY; lest any of you be hardened through the deceitfulness of sin. For we are made partakers of Christ, if we hold the beginning of our confidence steadfast unto the end; While it is said, TODAY IF YE WILL HEAR His VOICE, HARDEN NOT YOUR HEARTS, AS IN THE PROVOCATION. For some, when they had heard, did provoke: howbeit not all that came out of Egypt by Moses. But with whom was He grieved forty years? Was it not with them that had sinned, whose carcasses fell in the wilderness? And to whom sware He that they should not enter into His rest, but to them that believed not? So we see that they could not enter in because of unbelief. LET us therefore fear, lest, a promise being left us of entering into His rest, any of you should seem to come short of it. For unto us was the gospel preached, as well as unto them: but the word preached did not profit them, not being mixed with faith in them that heard it. For we which have believed do enter into rest, as He said, As I HAVE SWORN IN MY WRATH, IF THEY SHALL ENTER INTO MY REST: although the works were finished from the foundation of the world. For He spake in a certain place of the seventh day on this wise, AND GOD DID REST THE SEVENTH DAY FROM ALL His WORKS. And in this place again, IF THEY SHALL ENTER INTO MY REST. Seeing therefore it remaineth that some must enter therein, and they to whom it was first preached entered not in because of unbelief: Again, He limiteth a certain day, saying in David, TODAY, after so long a time; as it is said, TODAY IF YE WILL HEAR His VOICE, HARDEN NOT YOUR HEARTS. For if Jesus had given them rest, then would He not afterward have spoken of another day. There remaineth therefore a rest to the people of God. For He that is entered into His rest, He also hath ceased from His own works, as God did from his. Let us labor therefore to enter into that rest, lest any man fall after the same example of unbelief. For the word of God is quick, and powerful, and sharper than any two-edged sword, piercing even to the dividing asunder of soul and spirit, and of the joints and marrow, and is a discerner of the thoughts and intents of the heart. Neither is there any creature that is not manifest in His sight: but all things are naked and opened unto the eyes of Him with whom we have to do" (Hebrews 3:7-19; 4:1-13).

**Discussion Questions:**

1. **In what ways can you find rest in the Lord?**

2. **Do you rest in your spirit, or are you fighting the will of the flesh?**

3. **When do you know when enough is enough and you can rest in the Lord?**

4. **At what point do you rule and reign over sin?**

5. **Is everybody comfortable with sin in your circle? Do you find yourself joining them since you can't win them over?**

6. **When do you stand for Christ and tell people what is true according to the Word?**

**Points to Discuss: After reading the lesson, go back and answer the questions in the lesson for an in-depth discussion.**

**Notes:**

## LESSON 11

# What Do I Profit by Being Here (What is My Mission)?

**Foundation: Hebrews 10:11-39**

*"And every priest standeth daily ministering and offering oftentimes the same sacrifices, which can never take away sins: but this man, after He had offered one sacrifice for sins forever, sat down on the right hand of God; from henceforth expecting till His enemies be made His footstool. For by one offering He hath perfected forever them that are sanctified. Whereof the Holy Ghost also is a witness to us: for after that He had said before, THIS IS THE COVENANT THAT I WILL MAKE WITH THEM AFTER THOSE DAYS, SAITH THE LORD, I WILL PUT MY LAWS INTO THEIR HEARTS, AND IN THEIR MINDS WILL I WRITE THEM; AND THEIR SINS AND INIQUITIES WILL I REMEMBER NO MORE. Now where remission of these is, there is no more offering for sin. Having therefore, brethren, boldness to enter into the holiest by the blood of Jesus, by a new and living way, which He hath consecrated for us, through the veil, that is to say, His flesh; And having a high priest over the house of God; let us draw near with a true heart in full assurance of faith, having our hearts sprinkled from an evil conscience, and our bodies washed with pure water. Let us hold fast the profession of our faith without wavering; (for He is faithful that promised), and let us consider one another to provoke unto love and to good works: not forsaking the assembling of ourselves together, as the manner of some is; but exhorting one another, and so much the more, as ye see the day approaching. For if we sin willfully after that we have received the knowledge of the truth, there remaineth*

*no more sacrifice for sins, but a certain fearful looking for of judgment and fiery indignation, which shall devour the adversaries. He that despised Moses' law died without mercy under two or three witnesses: Of how much sorer punishment, suppose ye, shall he be thought worthy, who hath trodden under-foot the Son of God, and hath counted the blood of the covenant, wherewith he was sanctified, an unholy thing, and hath done despite unto the Spirit of grace? For we know Him that hath said, VENGEANCE BELONGETH UNTO ME, I WILL RECOMPENSE, saith the Lord. And again, THE LORD SHALL JUDGE His PEOPLE. It is a fearful thing to fall into the hands of the living God. But call to remembrance the former days, in which, after ye were illuminated, ye endured a great fight of afflictions; Partly, whilst ye were made a gazing stock both by reproaches and afflictions; and partly, whilst ye became companions of them that were so used. For ye had compassion of me in my bonds, and took joyfully the spoiling of your goods, knowing in yourselves that ye have in heaven a better and an enduring substance. Cast not away therefore your confidence, which hath great recompense of reward. For ye have need of patience, that, after ye have done the will of God, ye might receive the promise. FOR YET A LITTLE WHILE, AND He THAT SHALL COME WILL COME, AND WILL NOT TARRY. NOW THE JUST SHALL LIVE BY FAITH: BUT IF ANY MAN DRAW BACK, MY SOUL SHALL HAVE NO PLEASURE IN HIM. But we are not of them who draw back unto perdition; but of them that believe to the saving of the soul."*

### A. Fighting for the Faith

Hold on to the good fight of faith, knowing that your heavenly Father endured enough for you to have a right to the tree of life. As long as you go through this lifetime, know that God activates by faith and good substance. Do not lay up treasures for yourselves here on earth, but focus on the heavenly realm of God. He has your sacrifices and best interest in mind. Do good, and seek the Lord sending up timber to heaven so God can reward you there. Remember Christ's death is sanctification of things we should have here on earth. The earth is the Lord's and the fullness thereof. When you bless and serve someone on this earthly side, God will make room for you to be greatly rewarded in heaven. He will open doors for you that no man can close. He will give you room to enjoy the greater things in life while He is being glorified. "Wisdom is the principal thing; therefore get wisdom: and with all thy getting get understanding" (Proverbs 4:7).

Once He has opened the doors for you to prosper, do not be greedy but have a good level head to think ahead and to be ready for the next move of God. He is ready to do marvelous things for you. "Rejoice, and be exceeding glad: for great is your reward in heaven; for so persecuted they the prophets which were before you" (Matthew 5:12). "Lay not up for yourselves treasures upon earth, where moth and rust doth corrupt, and where thieves break through and steal: But lay up for yourselves treasures in heaven, where neither moth nor rust doth corrupt, and where thieves do not break through nor steal, for where your treasure is, there will your heart be also" (Matthew 6:19-21). God will bless you according to your merits in heaven. Don't delay, read the word and pray daily.

### B. Worship God in Spirit and in Truth

"Ye worship ye know not what: we know what we worship: for salvation is of the Jews. But the hour cometh, and now is, when the true worshipers shall worship the Father in spirit and in truth: for the Father seeketh such to worship him. God is a Spirit: and they that worship Him must worship Him in spirit and in truth" (John 4:22-24). People have gotten so complacent with the world's system. We find ourselves satisfying the outer appearance, the flesh, and forgetting about the spiritual being. People fail to face reality about life. You may sugar coat it or make it seem that everything is alright and that all things are fine, but Jesus tells of a woman who had five husbands, only they were not her own. She chose the lifestyle to lie with or to entertain what supposedly belonged to someone else. As she had this conversation with Jesus, she found out that He's a greater being; He's the one that could satisfy all of her needs and wants. Not only can He whisper sweet nothings, but He can fulfill her spiritual being with what she has been missing all of her life, the things that she has been seeking other men to satisfy her with. Not only is He the confidante, but He is the Great I Am and merciful God. He can fulfill the innermost desires of our hearts. He has the right and final say.

### C. Repentance

You know, people these days will get upset with you when you say something about their personal life and how they are living or treating others. They are quick to point out your downfalls and what you are doing, but have a hard time with the reality of themselves. Although this may be the case, our God is more than enough. He is going to bring it all back to their remembrance. He is going to make it all come back so that people can see their lives as a motion picture. They will actually experience everything over again. People have gotten complacent with cheating, lying, stealing and living lies. Little do they realize that God sees all and knows all. When you bring a person's past to their remembrance, they tend to shoot it down and act as if it never happened, never trying to make it right with the person they hurt; they just cover their own feelings and desires. God is getting so fed up with selfish desires and intuitions from men that He is forming latitude of greatness and forgiveness at everybody's forefront. Once we begin to repent, repent, and repent again, then will we be able to see and hear from God. "I tell you, nay: but, except ye repent, ye shall all likewise perish" (Luke 13:3).

### D. What Are Your Thoughts About Life?

Time is drawing nigh for us to get it together. Either we're saved for real or not. Either we're going to live for Christ or die in hell for satisfying our flesh. No, it's not alright to lay up with somebody else when you or that person is married to someone else. It's not alright to lay up with somebody even if you're single. We must remember that God sits up high and looks down low. He even knows our thoughts before we think it. He knows if we're real or if we're fake. He knows our attitude and gratitude in life. What are you thinking – is it about your own selfish gains; is it how you can acquire more than the next person; is it how you can get even with somebody else? Do you go around using people for your own self-worth and leave them high and dry, never to look back and think about what have you done to them mentally or physically? Do you get what you want from people and not think about the barrier it has on their household or themselves? Are you greedy for money, clothes, hairstyles, or other selfish desires, and do not think about how your selfish desires destroy other homes? Do you care about the countless people you've destroyed due to your own selfish gain, just to get what you want? Do you get tired of how other people see you? Do people tend to complain about your selfish ways and attitude? Check yourself, and ask the Lord for a cleansing to be real with yourself.

It's okay to do a self-inventory. Get it right with God and you'll stop blaming everybody else for your faults and downfall. It's not everybody else's fault that you didn't do what you wanted to do in life. Take responsibility for yourself. Ask the Lord to purge you with hyssop, and He'll make you whiter than snow. "HAVING therefore these promises, dearly beloved, let us cleanse ourselves from all filthiness of the flesh and spirit, perfecting holiness in the fear of God" (2 Corinthians 7:1). "Come now, and let us reason together, saith the Lord: though your sins be as scarlet, they shall be as white as snow: though they be red like crimson, they shall be as woo. If ye be willing and obedient, ye shall eat the good of the land: but if ye refuse and rebel, ye shall be devoured with the sword: for the mouth of the Lord hath spoken it" (Isaiah 1:18-20).

**E. What Is Your Purpose?**

What is your purpose here on earth? God has a plan for all of our lives. Either we are going to tap into His plan or keep chasing our own feeble minds for our own selfish desires and greed. What have you done for God lately? Are you living to please God or man? Is your life in vain? Did you hurt someone and felt like you got even with them? Did you acquire selfish gain for you and only you? Did you try to make it right with someone else? Did you try to get even because of a past hurt or failure? Are you living for you or Christ? Christ wants to be first in all that you say and do. Our actions speak louder than words. We need to allow our spiritual man to lead and guide us in the path of righteousness. Have you read the Word to feed your spirit? Have you read the Word to hear a word from God? Do you seek God in spirit and in truth? Reading the Word to feed your spirit is the ultimate way to get God's attention because in His Word are many facets of what He desires from you. He wants you to be real and keep it right for Him. "But seek ye first the kingdom of God, and His righteousness; and all these things shall be added unto you" (Matthew 6:33). Mean what you say, and say what you mean. "A good man out of the good treasure of His heart bringeth forth that which is good; and an evil man out of the evil treasure of His heart bringeth forth that which is evil; for of the abundance of the heart His mouth speaketh" (Luke 6:45).

What are you doing that is pleasing in God's sight? How are you living? Are you real, or are you fake? What have you done for God lately? What's your true passion in life? What are you reading and praying about? What are you watching on television and/or technical device, is it pleasing in God's sight? Is it real; is it for or about Jesus? Are you talking or preaching one thing and living a totally different life? Do you constantly lie to make things seem right to justify yourself? Is it that everybody dislikes you because you're who you are? It's not always everybody else; sometimes you need to check yourself. Get it right with God. Worship God in Spirit and Truth. Stop trying to fit in with others. Stop pacifying and finding favor in man. Man doesn't have a heaven or hell to put you in, but God does. He has the ultimate say in our well being of life. Misery loves company, but God favors the upright and Just man. Either you'll live for Him or die in sin. What's your life plan – life in Christ or death?"For to me to live is Christ, and to die is gain. But if I live in the flesh, this is the fruit of my labor: yet what I shall choose I wot not. For I am in a strait betwixt two, having a desire to depart, and to be with Christ; which is far better" (Philippians 1:21-23). "And they that are Christ's have crucified the flesh with the affections and lusts. If we live in the Spirit, let us also walk in the Spirit. Let us not be desirous of vain glory, provoking one another, envying one another" (Galatians 5:24-26).

**Discussion Questions:**

1. **What is your mission on earth?**

2. **Do you believe there will be heaven here on earth?**

3. **Do you believe that there is an afterlife?**

4. **Are you preparing yourself for a heavenly life?**

5. **Do you believe in the "Lamb's Book of Life?" If so, how do you view it? If not, why not?**

6. **What does repentance mean to you?**

7. **Is it okay to live as you please now, while believing that God will forgive you of your sins at the last minute or whenever you feel like repenting?**

8. **How are you truly living, knowing that God sees and knows all?**

**9. Will there be a story to tell about what you've done in the dark?**

**10. Are you serving your purpose and working for the Lord?**

**Points to Discuss: After reading the lesson, go back and answer the questions in the lesson for an in-depth discussion.**

**Notes:**

## LESSON 12

# He Who Has an Ear to Hear, Let Him Hear

**Foundation: Revelation 2:7; 3:7-13**

*"He that hath an ear, let Him hear what the Spirit saith unto the churches; to Him that overcometh will I give to eat of the tree of life, which is in the midst of the paradise of God. And to the angel of the church in Philadelphia write; 'These things saith He that is holy, He that is true, He THAT HATH THE KEY OF DAVID, HE THAT OPENETH, AND NO MAN SHUTTETH; AND SHUTTETH, AND NO MAN OPENETH; I know thy works: behold, I have set before thee an open door, and no man can shut it: for thou hast a little strength, and hast kept my word, and hast not denied my name. Behold, I will make them of the synagogue of Satan, which say they are Jews, and are not, but do lie; behold, I will make them to come and worship before thy feet, and to know that I have loved Thee. Because thou hast kept the word of my patience, I also will keep Thee from the hour of temptation, which shall come upon all the world, to try them that dwell upon the earth. Behold, I come quickly: hold that fast which thou hast, that no man take thy crown, Him that overcometh will I make a pillar in the temple of my God, and He shall go no more out: and I will write upon Him the name of my God, and the name of the city of my God, which is new Jerusalem, which cometh down out of heaven from my God: and I will write upon Him my new name. He that hath an ear, let Him hear what the Spirit saith unto the churches."*

### A. When Trials Come, Will You Stand?

God is soon to come, and though your trials may seem difficult, uncontrollable, or in disarray, hold on and know that the testing of your faith will cause you to be strong. Everyone goes through trials and tribulations, but a lot of people don't know to hold on to God's unchanging hand. The testing of your faith produces patience, perseverance, understanding, and the preservation of your Love for Jesus Christ. The more you stay in the Word, the more you will know and understand the reason that you experience the things that you do. If you look to your left and to your right, everyone is not still standing; everyone does not have faith and truly believe that God is ***El Shaddai***, the All Sufficient God. No one will see life for what it is worth if He does not keep His eyes on the promise of God. You may think of circumstances and situations where you do not feel loved and appreciated, but you must look beyond people to see the Lord.

### B. Guard Your Heart in Your Marriage

This is especially true in marriage. The enemy loves to kick us when he thinks we're down and out, particularly when we feel that we cannot sink any lower. It is during these times when he often will use our loved ones to hurt us. The enemy may say that our loved one (significant other) does not care or that he or she may wish they were with someone else other than you, but little do they know the grass is not greener on the other side. God has a way of bringing things back to their remembrance; that is when they realize that what they had was truly a gift from God. Things may not be as they thought they would be because they were dipping and dabbling with fleshly lusts and not seeking God. "Dearly beloved, I beseech you as strangers and pilgrims; abstain from fleshly lusts, which war against the soul" (1 Peter 2:11).

See the enemy does not want you to be happy. He wants to always keep that negative image at the forefront of your life just to remind you from whence you came. He will keep that lustful image there just to remind you that there is a place you will always want to remain. But when you keep your mind stayed on Jesus, He will bring it to pass that He is the keeper and wants you to worship him. He wants your power and mind focused on Him because He will keep you in perfect peace. "Thou wilt keep him in perfect peace, whose mind is stayed on Thee: because he trusteth in Thee. Trust ye in the Lord forever: for in the Lord Jehovah is everlasting strength" (Isaiah 26:3, 4).

## C. Have You Encountered God?

In order to be more like Jesus, to look and act more like Jesus, you got to put on the whole armor of God so that you will be able to stand against the wiles of the devil (Ephesians 6:11). You got to seek Him by fasting, praying, and reading the Word. Once you have had an encounter with him, you will never be the same, you will never respond the same, and you will never act the same. You must establish a true relationship with God by seeking Him now that He may be found. No woman or man can satisfy that innermost desire that you have better than God. You can search high and low for a Mister or Miss Feel Good, Look Good, and Sex You Up Good, but only God has the power to supply all of your needs according to His riches in glory.

There may be times when you are thinking of how people mistreat you, use you, or talk about and persecute you, but just hold on to God's unchanging hand. You cannot fight every battle that comes your way. You cannot stop people from talking about you. You cannot make people like or Love you. In order to get over those types of resentments, you must stay focused and keep the faith knowing that God knows your heart, mind, body and soul. Jeremiah 1:5 says, "Before I formed thee in the belly I knew thee; and before thou camest forth out of the womb I sanctified thee, and I ordained thee a prophet unto the nations." He is the only person that knows you. Nobody can do you like Jesus. Nobody can sustain and uplift you like Jesus. Nobody can give you peace of mind like Jesus. Nobody can understand you like Jesus. Hold on and wait a while. "For yet a little while, and He that shall come will come, and will not tarry" (Hebrews 10:37). He who will keep you is watching over you now. He knows your thoughts before you think it. "Humble yourselves therefore under the mighty hand of God, that He may exalt you in due time: Casting all your care upon him; for He careth for you" (1 Peter 5:6, 7). If you cast your cares on Him, He will bring everything to pass and establish you into His being. Hold on, and wait on the Lord. He will never leave you nor forsake you. "Rest in the Lord, and wait patiently for him: fret not thyself because of Him who prospereth in His way, because of the man who bringeth wicked devices to pass" (Psalm 37:7).

**Discussion Questions:**

1. **Have you ever fallen into fleshly lust? If so, how did you overcome?**

2. **Is it important or necessary to repent when you commit a sin?**

3. **How do you handle people that mistreat or misuse you?**

4. **Do you feel like it is rewarding or beneficial to fast and pray?**

5. **When do you know that you've had an encounter with God?**

6. **Do you cast your cares on Christ and leave them there?**

**Points to Discuss: After reading the lesson, go back and answer the questions in the lesson for an in-depth discussion.**

**Notes:**

## LESSON 13

# *Thirsting for God*

**Foundation: John 4:1-42**

*"WHEN therefore the Lord knew how the Pharisees had heard that Jesus made and baptized more disciples than John, though Jesus himself baptized not, but His disciples, He left Judea, and departed again into Galilee. And He must needs go through Samaria. Then cometh He to a city of Samaria, which is called Sychar, near to the parcel of ground that Jacob gave to his son Joseph. Now Jacob's well was there. Jesus therefore, being wearied with His journey, sat thus on the well: and it was about the sixth hour. There cometh a woman of Samaria to draw water: Jesus saith unto her, 'Give Me to drink.' (For His disciples were gone away unto the city to buy meat). Then saith the woman of Samaria unto Him, 'How is it that Thou, being a Jew, askest drink of me, which am a woman of Samaria? For the Jews have no dealings with the Samaritans.' Jesus answered and said unto her, 'If thou knewest the gift of God, and who it is that saith to thee, Give Me to drink; thou wouldest have asked of Him, and He would have given thee living water.' The woman saith unto Him, 'Sir, Thou hast nothing to draw with, and the well is deep: from whence then hast Thou that living water? Art Thou greater than our father Jacob, which gave us the well, and drank thereof himself, and his children, and his cattle? Jesus answered and said unto her, 'Whosoever drinketh of this water shall thirst again: But whosoever drinketh of the water that I shall give him shall never thirst; but the water that I shall give him shall be in him a well of water springing up into everlasting life.' The woman saith unto Him, 'Sir, give me give this water, that I thirst not, neither come hither to draw.' Jesus saith unto her, 'Go, call thy husband, and come hither'. The woman answered and said, 'I have no husband.' Jesus said unto her, 'Thou hast well*

*said, I have no husband: for thou hast had five husbands; and he whom thou now hast is not thy husband: in that saidst thou truly.' The woman saith unto Him, 'Sir, I perceive that Thou art a prophet. Our fathers worshiped in this mountain; and ye say that in Jerusalem is the place where men ought to worship.' Jesus saith unto her, 'Woman, believe Me, the hour cometh, when ye shall neither in this mountain, nor yet at Jerusalem, worship the Father. Ye worship ye know not what: we know what we worship: for salvation is of the Jews. But the hour cometh, and now is, when the true worshipers shall worship the Father in spirit and in truth: for the Father seeketh such to worship Him. God is a spirit: and they that worship Him must worship Him in spirit and in truth.' The woman saith unto Him, 'I know that Messiah cometh, which is called Christ: when He is come, He will tell us all things'. Jesus saith unto her, 'I that speak unto thee am He.' And upon this came His disciples, and marveled that He talked with the woman: yet no man said, 'What seekest Thou?' or, 'Why talkest Thou with her?' The woman then left her waterpot, and went her way into the city, and saith to the men, 'Come, see a man, which told me all things that ever I did: is not this the Christ?' Then they went out of the city, and came unto Him. In the mean while His disciples prayed Him, saying, 'Master, eat.' But He said unto them, 'I have meat to eat that ye know not of.' Therefore said the disciples one to another, 'Hath any man brought Him aught to eat?' Jesus saith unto them, 'My meat is to do the will of Him that sent Me, and to finish His work. Say not ye, There are yet four months, and then cometh harvest? Behold, I say unto you, lift up your eyes, and look on the fields; for they are white already to harvest. And he that reapeth receiveth wages, and gathereth fruit unto life eternal: that both he that soweth and he that reapeth may rejoice together. And herein is that saying true, One soweth, and another reapeth. I sent you to reap that whereon ye bestowed no labor: other men labored, and ye are entered into their labors.' And many of the Samaritans of that city believed on Him for the saying of the woman, which testified, 'He told me all that ever I did.' So when the Samaritans were come unto Him, they besought Him that He would tarry with them: and He abode there two days. And many more believed because of His own word; And said unto the woman, 'Now we believe, not because of thy saying: for we have heard Him ourselves, and know that this is indeed the Christ, the Savior of the world.'*

### A. Is God Calling You?

Jesus told the Samaritan woman that He would give her living water, springing up into everlasting life. To desire, hunger, and thirst for God is what He required of her. Like the

Samaritan woman at the well, Jesus is telling us to desire, hunger, and thirst for Him. Instead of allowing your tears to remind you about him; ask yourself; "Where is my God?" We are in a time in which we need to know, should want to know, and must know about Jesus. No one or nothing should be able to separate you from the Love of God. There are situations that may seem dim or negative, but when you hold onto His unchanging hand and see and believe that you've been in His presence, you'll never be the same. In order to feel His presence, in order to have a close encounter with Him, you must first seek Him and allow Him to come into your life. "Ask, and it shall be given you; seek, and ye shall find; knock, and it shall be opened unto you" (Matthew 7:7). God wants you, but_you must let Him come in. He said that when He comes in, He will be your dwelling place. He will make your narrow place straight. He will make everything alright if you allow Him to have His way with you and your life. The secret is giving God your all in all. If you allow Him to dwell in your presence, you will never be the same. You will see the true meaning and picture of life. He will show you the things that He can do for and will give to you. When you seek God with the purest and utmost faithfulness of your mind, body and soul, He will show you things you never thought you would see before.

### B. Who is the Inner Me?

Man's problem and drawback from God is his pride, his reliance upon his own strength, and his refusal to rely upon God; it may mess up his manly image for people to know that he has been in God's presence. We think to ourselves, "I cannot let people see me cry because they will think I am weak. I cannot take off this mask because they will see the true me, the inner me. I must keep up my guards because I don't want people to see who I really am and how I am. I want to keep the façade going. I want to keep the hype right just for me." Get your man-made, mighty, Superman self together by giving your complete being to God. Only He can make you who you really are. He can show you how and what He wants you to be. You will never have to struggle another day in your life. You will never have to wonder what is going on in your life. Sometimes you are your own hindrance. If you would give yourself fully to Jesus, you would never have to wonder and worry about the carnal things because God would bring it all to pass. He will make your enemy your footstool. Let Him come in. But once you allow Him to come in, you must totally surrender to him. Keep your mind stayed on Him. Pray to Him, and talk to Him. Read His Word; learn it, know it, grasp it, and let Him reveal the true Him to you. You will never be the same, in Jesus' name.

Meet with God daily. Not in a two minute prayer, but sit down, and turn off the TV and other distractions. Get on your knees, or lay prostrate before Him, and have a divine moment of meditation with Him. He will take you to a place you have never been before. He will allow you to enter into the inner courts and go behind the veil. This is a place that you can truly worship Him like never before. Prepare yourself for a true encounter with Christ, "which hope we have as an anchor of the soul, both sure and steadfast, and which entereth into that within the veil" (Hebrews 6:19).

**Discussion Questions:**

1. **How do you know that you're thirsty for God?**

2. **Is God supplying all of your needs, or are you relying on other sources?**

3. **Who is the inner you?**

4. **What does the inner you look like to Christ?**

5. **Have you given God all of yourself?**

6. **Would you die to yourself for Christ?**

**Points to Discuss: After reading the lesson, go back and answer the questions in the lesson for an in-depth discussion.**

**Notes:**

# LESSON 14

# *Identifying Dry Spots*

**Foundation: John 7:37-39**

*"In the last day, that great day of the feast, Jesus stood and cried, saying, 'If any man thirst, let him come unto Me, and drink. He that believeth on Me, as the scripture hath said, out of his belly shall flow rivers of living water. (But this spake He of the Spirit, which they that believe on Him should receive: for the Holy Ghost was not yet given; because that Jesus was not yet glorified.)"*

## A. Are You Surrendered to His Presence?

If anyone thirsts (desires, longs to be with, longs to have an intimate relationship, wants to be like Him and not like man, wants to know that you know Him without a shadow of a doubt, wants to be in a close relationship and bond with Him, wants to hear His voice, wants to be in His presence, wants to go behind the veil, wants to be where you will know that you have been in the presence of the Lord), the Lord says, "Come to Me and drink." You will know without a shadow of doubt when you have been in the presence of the Lord because the Great I Am is a matchless God that no man can place in a box. He cannot be bought with a price because He is priceless, and He has already paid the price for the sin of the world. He wants to be in your life. God desires for all of us, not just a few saints, to be saved, sanctified, and filled with the Holy Ghost. He wants us to have a divine relationship with Him. Just as the scripture says, "He that believeth on Me, as the scripture hath said, out of his heart shall flow rivers of living water" (John 7:38).

Can you imagine the ultimate way of being in that state? Since we do not give God our all, we limit Him to giving us just a taste of what He can and will do for us. In order to receive abundant blessings, you have to be willing to take a leap of faith. You must be in a position where you can, and will, ask the Lord to lead and guide your daily walk. Every day must become assigned decisions made according to the Lord. In order to thirst for God, we must be in a fetal position where it is no more "me and I," but God. It must come to the point at which you are not struggling to see, know, and hear everything from yourself but from God. Once you let go and let God, you will see a change and a shifting in the atmosphere. Things will never be the same because you will have allowed Him to have the final say of where you are and where you are going. Christ is looking evermore at the pictures of our lives and at the places He would have us to be, in the place of having more than enough. We must position ourselves to feel and know that He is God, and He is God all by Himself.

**B. Are You Praying Without Ceasing?**

It is time that we get into a praying mentality in which we pray without ceasing for all things – not just when trouble comes, not just when things are dim, not just when we think we need something, and not just when we think we ought to; we should pray at all times. God is seeking those true worshippers. He said, "But the hour cometh, and now is, when the true worshipers shall worship the Father in spirit and in truth: for the Father seethes such to worship him. God is a spirit: and, they that worship Him must worship Him in spirit and in truth" (John 4:23, 24). God wants us to be real. He wants our entire spirit, mind, body and soul. You will only get a glimpse of His glory if you give a little, but you can get a full mental picture of a true and living God with the ultimate release of your faith towards Him, which comes as a result of a life fully submitted in prayer. He will open up doors that no man can close. He will make your narrow way straight. No longer will you "sink or swim" in life. You will always swim because God knows your heart. He knows your thoughts even before you think it, so why not share your thoughts with your heavenly Father in prayer? What are you waiting for? If you are longing for God, find Him while you still have time.

**Discussion Questions:**

**1. Can you identify dry spots in your life?**

2. **How do you heal dry spots in your life?**

3. **Do you have to go through circumstances to thirst for God?**

4. **How can you aid someone you identify who is thirsting for God?**

5. **How do you know when there is a spiritual change in your life?**

6. **Does praying without ceasing mean praying in only one spot? Are you praying without ceasing?**

**Points to Discuss: After reading the lesson, go back and answer the questions in the lesson for an in-depth discussion.**

**Notes:**

# LESSON 15

# *Hope in God*

**Foundation: Psalm 42:1-6**

*"As the hart panteth after the water brooks, so panteth my soul after Thee, O God. My soul thirsteth for God, for the living God: when shall I come and appear before God? My tears have been my meat day and night, while they continually say unto me, 'Where is thy God?' When I remember these things, I pour out my soul in me: for I had gone with the multitude. I went with them to the house of God, with the voice of joy and praise, with a multitude that kept holyday. Why art thou cast down, O my soul? And why art thou disquieted in me? Hope thou in God: for I shall yet praise Him for the help of His countenance. O my God, my soul is cast down within me: therefore will I remember Thee from the land of Jordan, and of the Hermonites, from the hill Mizar."*

## A. Pray Like David Prayed

In a time of trouble, we need to cry out to God like David. A modern version of David's cry would sound something like this: "God, when I remember how I've cried out to You in my time of distress and disappointment, I think back to the time when I desired and yearned for only you because only you could see me through. God, morning by morning, new mercies I see. I'm still looking for a divine visitation from You as I thirst and hunger after Your righteousness, and as I continue to lean and depend on You for greater days and promises ahead. As I walk in Your heavenly places, the saints are chanting for You, the saints are yearning for a relationship with You that is mightier than ever. I ask that You grant me the inspiration, the motivation, the zeal, and the tenacity to walk in Your grace and mercy that is so sufficient for me. I want to take back everything the devil has stolen from me. I want to walk in uprightness. I want to move and breathe in the anointing. I want to be just like You."

**B. Put Your Trust in the Lord**

The following is a prayer I've prayed to the Lord when I needed to put my trust in Him. "I no longer put my trust in man because I know they will fail me, but once I see, feel and touch Your presence and anointing, there are greater days ahead that I see. The road may seem rough and dim, but I know You have all power in Your hands, and that no weapon formed against me shall prosper. Everything You have placed before me shall come to pass. Although the enemy can try to steal, kill, destroy, and devour everything that comes my way, I know that he cannot succeed if I am fully equipped with the whole armor of God–the Word, prayer, and fasting. When I read your Word, Lord, You give me a divine revelation every time, just to remind me that I am Your child and that when things are getting bad, it is actually getter better. Lord, that you would save, sanctify, deliver and set free this entire household is my prayer. Now greater mercies I see as You equip each of us to live truthfully, humbly, and righteously before You. Thank You, Lord Jesus!"

**C. Do You Have a Relationship With God?**

The foundation scriptures for this lesson reflect on when the Psalmist went to the house of worship with the saints to praise and worship God. But now, he is in distress, he is numb, and he feels a dry spell in which he cannot find God. They asked him, "Where is your God?" Although his soul is cast down and quieted, he will still praise and worship Him. He will focus on remembering God way back when, from the hilltops and the valleys, but most of all when God had His spirit and soul in high places. Right now, he is dry and needs to hear a word from God. We all get to a ***dry place*** in our lives when we ourselves wonder where God is, what we are doing, if we are in His will, if we are living right, if we are willing to do what He wants us to do, if we are truly being led by God, or if we are leading ourselves. These are questions we ask ourselves when we are going through. God allows this dry season to come in order for us to get back into His presence so that we can get into a deeper relationship with Him. God wishes most of all that we become His true conquerors and that we continuously walk in the spirit realm because that allows us to always be open and submissive to Him. He is a great and merciful God.

**Discussion Questions:**

1. **What are you hoping for and seeking God about?**

2. **Where do you want God to take you at this point in life?**

3. **What are you doing to get where you want to be?**

4. **What is a "dry place" in your life?**

5. **Have you ever sought after God and were not fulfilled? What did you think and do?**

6. **When has God showed Himself merciful to you?**

**Points to Discuss: After reading the lesson, go back and answer the questions in the lesson for an in-depth discussion.**

**Notes:**

LESSON 16

# *Alive With God, Alive in Christ*

**Foundation: Romans 5:8; Ephesians 2:1-6**

*"But God commendeth His love toward us, in that, while we were yet sinners, Christ died for us" (Romans 5:8).*

*"And you hath He quickened, who were dead in trespasses and sins; Wherein in time past ye walked according to the course of this world, according to the prince of the power of the air, the spirit that now worketh in the children of disobedience: Among whom also we all had our conversation in times past in the lusts of our flesh, fulfilling the desires of the flesh and of the mind; and were by nature the children of wrath, even as others. But God, who is rich in mercy, for His great love wherewith He loved us, Even when we were dead in sins, hath quickened us together with Christ, (by grace ye are saved;) And hath raised us up together, and made us sit together in heavenly places in Christ Jesus" (Ephesians 2:1-6).*

## A. Focus Yourself on Christ

When Christ died for all of our sins, the sin of the world, it was up to us to seek and to desire Him because of our thankfulness and gratitude. It was because of His grace and mercy that we now have a place at the table in this life; however, our selfish ways, our disbelief, and our believing that we've made ourselves who we are have become the roots of our problems. We have deceived ourselves by thinking that we are our own persons and don't need Christ at the center of our lives. We as believers have to change our mindsets and focus on Christ. If it wasn't for Christ's grace and mercy, we wouldn't be where we are today. Man has no control or power to place us anywhere; it's all God's doing. God has a way of reminding us where we are and where we should be, but our ultimate focus should be to be like Him and in His image.

**B. Die Daily to the Flesh**

We should constantly die to the flesh and ask the spirit man to rise in us. We are just as wrong as the next person when we don't seek God and His well-being in our lives. We are to walk divinely according to God's grace and mercy. We should seek to establish a relationship with Him so that it will be easier for us to know what He wants and deems for our lives. As we continue on this journey, if we are not where we want to be in Christ, it is our responsibility to draw closer to Him. James 4:8 tells us, "Draw nigh to God, and He will draw nigh to you." Even if we are close to Him, we still need to seek Him and His being. We should desire to have our thoughts like His thoughts and not our own. Some of us are selfish; we want everything to go our way. We want everything to be done like we want it. If people don't say what we want them to say, do what we want them to do, or dress and act as we would have them to dress and act, then they don't fit in with our circle, or we just don't like them. That is selfish, inconsiderate, and ungodly.

God is the only person we are to please and satisfy. We are to accept everybody as they are and as whom they are. We are our own enemies because of our little gods, which we have within us. Sometimes people get to the point where they think they own everything and everybody, but this is wrong. Only God can change a person's mindset and mentality. He's the only one that can change the way a person behaves. Sometimes we are not aware of our constant complaints, disbelief, bad attitudes, and selfishness toward others. It takes a closer walk and desire to be like God for us to see our own faults and weaknesses. When we focus on Christ for who He is and face our enemy (self-righteousness), it's then that we can begin to live life according to the Lord and His desires and riches.

**C. Are You a Follower of Christ?**

God is seeking obedient believers, not those that pacify and do it while we're in public, but those that look at Him for who He really is and who He demands us to be. God is waiting for true believers and followers. People get offended when their beliefs and walk with God are questioned. Is it because they are not sure of what they believe, or is it because they have hidden agendas and don't want to be exposed? Whatever it may be, God knows and sees all. He knows our thoughts, our desires, and what we are doing. Are you walking a true and faithful walk with Christ? If not, He knows the true you. He knows your thoughts, desires, and wants.

You must want Him, and you must want His ways in order to walk this life here on earth, in order to be a true Christian. Seek Christ and all of His ways. Worship Him, and read the Word. "Heaven and earth shall pass away, but my words shall not pass away" (Matthew 24:35).

**Discussion Questions:**

1. **What does it mean to be "alive with God, alive in Christ"?**

2. **Do you find yourself judging others? Is that of Christ?**

3. **Do you find yourself being selfish? Is that of Christ?**

4. **Was it a selfish act of God to die for our sins? Why or why not?**

5. **In what areas do you need to die to your flesh?**

6. **How do you know that you are a "true" follower of Christ?**

7. **Have you sinned since being a "saint?"**

**Points to Discuss: After reading the lesson, go back and answer the questions in the lesson for an in-depth discussion.**

**Notes:**

## LESSON 17

# *Withholding Nothing from God*

**Foundation: Deuteronomy 6:5; Matthew 22:37, 38**

*"And thou shalt love the Lord thy God with all tine heart, and with all thy soul, and with all thy might" (Deuteronomy 6:5).*

*"Jesus said unto him, THOU SHALT LOVE THY LORD THY GOD WITH ALL THY HEART, AND WITH ALL THY SOUL, AND WITH ALL THY MIND. This is the first and great commandment" (Matthew 22:37, 38).*

### A. Above All Else

To Love God with all of our hearts, souls, and minds is all that He asks of us. It doesn't seem impossible, but when you're living on earth daily, it becomes a challenge. You see, in order to Love God with all of your heart, body, soul, and mind means to get totally into Him. To give up yourself and be who He wants you to be is His greatest desire. It becomes a challenge when you're not aware of the fact that you Love some woman, man, child, material thing, earthly vessel, etc. more than you Love God. God wants all of you. He wants you to walk, talk, eat, sleep, and breathe Him. The more you seek Him, the more you desire Him. The more you seek that ultimate and intimate relationship with Him, the closer your walk and relationship becomes with Him. God wants our all in all. You can love other people and things, but nothing and no one should separate you from the Love of God. God wants our desire to be so great that the devil in hell can't even distract you. Even if the enemy comes in to destroy, he'll never succeed because the Master you so Love and desire has all power in His hands, and He can control everything. He'll protect you from the enemy and other things that are not of Him. Once your Love for Him has grown and is inseparable, then you'll know where your weaknesses and strengths lie in Him. The enemy comes to kill, steal, destroy, and devour, but nothing, absolutely nothing, should be able to separate you from the Love of God. "Be sober, be vigilant; because your adversary the devil, as a roaring lion, walketh about, seeking whom He may devour" (1 Peter 5:8).

**B. What Is Your Passion?**

You will know what replaces God in your heart when your passion and zeal for that thing begins to outweigh your passion and zeal for the things of God. Whatever you desire more than reading the word, praying, talking to God, talking about God, and living a righteous life, that thing has become your god. If you desire to do something else more than you desire to do any of the above situations, then God is no longer your God. God wants us to put Him first. There's nothing better than a God-fearing man or woman because their strongest desire is to seek Christ for who He is and to walk in His word and wisdom. Once you've been in the presence of God, your passion for Him will begin to ignite into a full-fledged fire; you'll never be the same. Just to hear from Him is awesome. Seek Him now while you still have time. Walk in His wisdom, and He'll open up doors for you that no man can close. Walk in His spirit and presence. God is Love.

**Discussion Questions:**

1. **Is it a challenge to hold back nothing from God?**

2. **Can you Love other people, animals, activities, or things more than you do God?**

3. **Is it a sin to Love others, animals or things more than Christ? Why or why not?**

4. **In what areas are you strong and what areas are you weak in Christ?**

5. **On a scale of 1-10, with 10 being the highest, rate your passion for Christ. Does your fire for Him need to be relit?**

6. **How do you walk in the word and wisdom of Christ?**

**Points to Discuss: After reading the lesson, go back and answer the questions in the lesson for an in-depth discussion.**

**Notes:**

# LESSON 18

# *Loving God Means Loving People*

**Foundation: Matthew 22:37-39; 1 Corinthians 13:1-8**

*"Jesus said unto him, THOU SHALT LOVE THE LORD THY GOD WITH ALL THY HEART, AND WITH ALL THY SOUL, AND WITH ALL THY MIND. This is the first and great commandment. And the second is like unto it, THOU SHALT LOVE THY NEIGHBOR AS THYSELF" (Matthew 22:37-39).*

*"Though I speak with the tongue of men and of angels, and have not charity, I am become as sounding brass, or a tinkling cymbal. And though I have the gift of prophecy, and understand all mysteries, and all knowledge; and though I have all faith, so that I could remove mountains, and have not charity, I am nothing. And though I bestow all my goods to feed the poor, and though I give my body to be burned, and have not charity, it profiteth me nothing. Charity suffereth long, and is kind; charity envieth not; charity vaunteth not itself, is not puffed up, Doth not behave itself unseemly, seeketh not her own, is not easily provoked, thinketh no evil; Rejoiceth not in iniquity, but rejoiceth in the truth; Beareth all things, believeth all things, hopeth all things, endureth all things. Charity never faileth: but whether there be prophecies, they shall fail; whether there be tongues, they shall cease; whether there be knowledge, it shall vanish away" (1 Corinthians 13:1-8).*

Love is the greatest gift and the first commandment of them all. But the commandment is not just to love God. God demands and orders us to Love our neighbors even as ourselves. The problem that most people have with this is that they can't get out of themselves. We have a problem seeing Love as the greatest and most precious gift because we're so wrapped up in our own worlds and who is doing something for us. Sometimes we form cliques with family members or people in our inner circles who we Love. Once we've formed "our world," we have a hard time reaching outside of the box.

Once upon a time, I used to think it was a cultural thing, but the more wisdom I acquire on a daily basis, I see that it is a "people thing." Even when I go out of town, I see the same thing. If you do not look, act, walk, or talk in a certain way, you do not fit in. If you do not agree with others, no matter how wrong they are, you just do not fit in. You see, people of today like compromise. They like agreeing with the wrong, even when they know it is supposed to be right. They like to pretend. If you walk a certain walk and do not conform to their ways, you are immediately cast out. This is a problem. You see, God's first and greatest commandment is to Love. If we are disobedient in Loving our neighbor as ourselves simply because they do fit into our man-made standards, we are out of His will. We must learn to Love unconditionally, unselfishly, without blame or dishonor. God wants us to Love those even when there is no Love in return, even when they are wrong, even when they literally hate your guts, even when you are just you, and even when they don't fit into our cliques. God's commandment is hard, especially when you know how people feel about you, but you must be obedient and do His will. God wants us to walk in His image, to be like Him, and to do His will. It's not hard when you look at it in this perspective; it's just that we must maintain His order.

The walk may be difficult, but it's well worth it in the end. To God be the glory. If we focus on Him and His ways, then we will understand that He has all power in His hands and is able to keep us from falling. In order to Love genuinely, you must stay prayed up, fasting and seeking God at all times. The walk becomes easier and easier. It'll never be an extremely easy task, but it is one that will show you just who you are in Christ. Follow Jesus! "Now unto Him that is able to keep you from falling, and to present you faultless before the presence of His glory with exceeding joy. To the only wise God our Savior, be glory and majesty, dominion and power, both now and ever. Amen" (Jude 24).

**Discussion Questions:**

1. **Can you Love outside of your clique or circle?**

2. **Can you see beyond your own needs to see the needs of others?**

3. **Can you Love a stranger unconditionally? What do you think about Jesus' story of the Good Samaritan (Luke 10:25-37)? Are you able to be the Good Samaritan for someone?**

4. **Can you Love someone after they've offended and/or hurt you?**

5. **Can you Love someone after they've hurt your child or another loved one?**

**Points to Discuss: After reading the lesson, go back and answer the questions in the lesson for an in-depth discussion.**

**Notes:**

## LESSON 19

# Yielding the Right of Way

**Foundation: Philippians 2:1-11**

*"If there be therefore any consolation in Christ, if any comfort of love, if any fellowship of the Spirit, if any bowels and mercies, Fulfill ye my joy, that ye be likeminded, having the same love, being of one accord, of one mind. Let nothing be done through strife or vainglory, but in lowliness of mind let each esteem other better than themselves. Look not every man on his own things, but every man also on the things of others. Let this mind be in you, which was also in Christ Jesus. Who, being in the form of God, thought it not robbery to be equal with God. But made Himself of no reputation, and took upon Him the form of a servant, and was made in the likeness of men: And being found in fashion as a man, He humbled Himself, and became obedient unto death, even the death of the cross. Wherefore God also hath highly exalted Him, and given Him a name which is above every name. That at the name of Jesus every knee should bow, of things in heaven, and things in earth, and things under the earth. And that every tongue should confess that Jesus Christ is Lord, to the glory of God the Father."*

### A. Humble Yourself to Receive His Grace

"But He giveth more grace. Wherefore He saith, God resisteth the proud, but giveth grace grace unto the humble" (James 4:6). When you are humble in Christ, nothing is impossible for God. God seeks us to be obedient servants who humble ourselves before His throne and are obedient to His word. Let the lowly brother speak or not have anything to say. Sometimes it's best to pray and not speak. Sometimes it's best to be humble and to let

God have His way. You should not have to tell people where you stand with Christ; your walk and your lifestyle should do the talking. Your humility with Christ should speak for itself. Sometimes it is confusing to see loud, flamboyant people go on and on about Christ, but as you continue to watch them closely, they are the very ones in whom you see the error of defense or sin All respect is labeled upon their attitude and gratitude. I tend to fade away from people who are too loud; they are audibly loud, but are their hearts in the right place? Is the root of their loudness a selfish desire to be seen and heard? These people depict to be more righteous than others, but their characters display something totally different.

It takes discipline, righteousness, self-examination, fasting, praying, and most of all, obedience to God to be humble. How can you be humble when you are talking so loudly saying the same thing over and over again, but you are double-minded in the same breath? You are only concerned with number one (yourself and "your world" around you). God knows your heart. He knows your thoughts before you think it. He knows your mindset and what game plan you are playing. Stop being loud if you are not truthful and not walking upright. God wants you to stop being phony when you know you do not mean what you are saying or doing. Stop being double-minded; that is a dangerous playing field. Stop all the "show" and be real. Humble yourself before the Lord, before His throne. He knows the true you. He knows the plans He has for your life. Seek God for real. Be real before the Lord. This is the true judgment of Christ. "Humble yourselves in the sight of the Lord, and He shall lift you up" (James 4:10). "Humble yourselves therefore under the mighty hand of God, that He may exalt you in due time" (1 Peter 5:6).

### B. Obedience

"But what think ye? A certain man had two sons; and he came to the first, and said, 'Son, go work today in my vineyard.' He answered and said, 'I will not'; but afterward He repented, and went. And he came to the second, and said likewise. And he answered and said, 'I go, sir': and went not. Whether of them twain did the will of his father?' They say unto Him, 'The first.' Jesus saith unto them, 'Verily I say unto you, that the publicans and the harlots go into the kingdom of God before you. For John came unto you in the way of righteousness, and ye believed him not: but the publicans and the harlots believed him: and ye, when ye had seen it, repented not afterward, that ye might believe him" (Matthew 21: 28-32).

Obedience is better than sacrifice. That is what we are to believe and keep at the forefront of God. Many saints have heard the voice of the Lord and complied with all that He told them to do, but there are still a great many that hear His voice, but are still reluctant to do His will. God is seeking people who will be obedient right now. He wants those who are radical enough to hear His voice and still be obedient enough to do His will. We tarry, sleep, and slumber for God, but are at a haste to do the will of men. Where are our priorities? God said that He will supply all of our needs according to His riches in glory. What are we waiting on? Why do we tarry? Why do we suffer long? What is the problem?

Some of us have a problem with others blessings and/or wealth. We get envious of what they have. Why? Did not God say He would supply all of your needs according to His riches in glory? "But my God shall supply all your need according to His riches in glory by Christ Jesus" (Philippians 4:19). He also said, "But they that wait upon the Lord shall renew their strength; they shall mount up with wings as eagles; they shall run, and not be weary; and they shall walk, and not faint" (Isaiah 40:31). Are you being obedient to wait upon the Lord as He prepares you for His blessings? Or are you spending your time being jealous of others' blessings? "Ye lust, and have not: ye kill, and desire to have, and cannot obtain: ye fight and war, yet ye have not, because ye ask not" (James 4:2). We have not because we ask not, and we are not obedient to His word and to His will. Put on the whole armor of God; seek His guidance, and see Him direct your path. When all is said and done, what are you waiting on to do His will? Why are you telling God okay yet still sitting there? If God allows you an opportunity to acquire power, wealth, dominion, and blessings according to His word and in His name, why are you still here, sitting on it? Bring out the powers from on high from within the inner you.

If God said it, that settles it. I do not care what He told you to do. Do it! It does not matter. Do not second guess Him. Do not underestimate Him. Let Him use you as His vessel and see it flourish. The enemy may try to deceive you, but pray without tarrying and see His faithful plea. "But without faith it is impossible to please Him: for he that cometh to God must believe that He is, and that He is a rewarder of them that diligently seek Him" (Hebrews 11:6). Wait on the Lord, and be of good courage. Be obedient to His will, and watch Him soar in your life. Amen! Amen! Amen!

**Discussion Questions:**

1. **Does humility merit favor with God?**

2. **What is a way that God has rewarded you because you were humble?**

3. **Do you ever look at the man in the mirror in judgment?**

4. **Can you identify your faults and repent?**

5. **What does it mean to be obedient to God?**

6. **Has God supplied all of your needs according to His riches in glory? Why or why not?**

7. **Are you fulfilling the works of the Lord in full obedience and not for selfish gains?**

8. **Have you done the will of the Father even when it was weird or uncomfortable?**

9. **When you've completed a mission for Christ, did you feel that he got the glory?**

**Points to Discuss: After reading the lesson, go back and answer the questions in the lesson for an in-depth discussion.**

**Notes:**

# LESSON 20

# *Blessings From God*

**Foundation: Malachi 3:8-18; 4:1-6; 2 Corinthians 8:1-15**

*"Will a man rob God? Yet ye have robbed me. But ye say, Wherein have we robbed Thee? In tithes and offerings. Ye are cursed with a curse: for ye have robbed me, even this whole nation. Bring ye all the tithes into the storehouse, that there may be meat in mine house, and prove me now herewith, saith the Lord of hosts, if I will not open you the windows of heaven, and pour you out a blessing, that there shall not be room enough to receive it. And I will rebuke the devourer for your sakes, and He shall not destroy the fruits of your ground; neither shall your vine cast her fruit before the time in the field, saith the Lord of hosts. And all nations shall call you blessed: for ye shall be a delightsome land, saith the Lord of hosts. Your words have been stout against me, saith the Lord. Yet ye say, What have we spoken so much against Thee? Ye have said, It is vain to serve God: and what profit is it that we have kept His ordinance, and that we have walked mournfully before the Lord of hosts? And now we call the proud happy; yea, they that work wickedness are set up; yea, they that tempt God are even delivered. Then they that feared the Lord spake often one to another; and the Lord hearkened, and heard it, and a book of remembrance was written before Him for them that feared the Lord, and that thought upon His name. And they shall be mine, saith the Lord of hosts, in that day when I make up my jewels; and I will spare them, as a man spareth His own son that serveth him. Then shall ye return, and discern between the righteous and the wicked, between Him that serveth God and Him that serveth Him not. FOR, behold, the day cometh, that shall burn as an oven; and all the proud, yea, and all that do wickedly, shall be stubble: and the day that cometh*

*shall turn them up, saith the Lord of hosts, that it shall leave them neither root nor branch. But unto you that fear my name shall the Sun of righteousness arise with healing in His wings; and y shall go forth, and grow up as calves of the stall. And ye shall tread down the wicked; for they shall be ashes under the soles of your feet in the day that I shall do this, saith the Lord of hosts. Remember ye the law of Moses my servant, which I commanded unto Him in Horeb for all Israel, with the statutes and judgments. Behold, I will send you Elijah the prophet before the coming of the great and dreadful day of the Lord: And He shall turn the heart of the fathers to the children, and the heart of the children to their fathers, lest I come and smite the earth with a curse" (Malachi 3:8-18; 4:1-6).*

*"Moreover, brethren, we do you to wit of the grace of God bestowed on the churches of Macedonia. How that in a great trial of affliction the abundance of their joy and their deep poverty abounded unto the riches of their liberality. For to their power, I bear record, yea, and beyond their power they were willing of themselves, Praying us with much entreaty that we would receive the gift, and take upon us the fellowship of the ministering to the saints. And this they did, not as we hoped, but first gave their own selves to the Lord, and unto us by the will of God. Insomuch that we desired Titus, that as He had begun, so He would also finish in you the same grace also. Therefore, as ye abound in everything, in faith, and utterance, and knowledge, and in all diligence, and in your love to us, see that ye abound in this grace also. I speak not by commandment, but by occasion of the forwardness of others, and to prove the sincerity of your love. For ye know the grace of our Lord Jesus Christ, that, though He was rich, yet for your sakes He became poor, that ye through His poverty might be rich. And herein I give my advice: for this is expedient for you, who have begun before, not only to do, but also to be forward a year ago. Now therefore perform the doing of it; that as there was a readiness to will, so there may be a performance also out of that which ye have. For if there be first a willing mind, it is accepted according to that a man hath, and not according to that He hath not. For I mean not that other men be eased, and ye burdened: But by an equality, that now at this time your abundance may be a supply for their want, that their abundance also may be a supply for your want: that there may be equality: As it is written, HE THAT HAD GATHERED MUCH HAD NOTHING OVER; AND He THAT HAD GATHERED LITTLE HAD NO LACK" (2 Corinthians 8:1-15).*

## A. Excel in Giving

God is waiting to bestow blessings upon blessings on the lives of His saints. He wants us to be blessed with a blessing and not cursed with a curse; however, there are stages we must follow in order to get to the place where He wants us to be. First of all, pray without ceasing, and ask for His guidance and leadership. Once you place Him at the center of your life, you will begin to see the blessings and things He has for you to do. Secondly, allow Him to use you like no other, not focusing on man and people with labels, but placing Him as your focal point and being obedient to His word, to His will, and to His way. He will open up the windows of heaven and pour out His blessings, but the ultimate way to receive this is by giving. You must learn to give in tithes and offerings, even when you do not think you have it to give. Giving in order to receive from God goes against the mindset of the world, but the Kingdom mindset requires us to sow a seed in order to reap a harvest. You must be spiritually minded and focused on the Lord. Do not place your concentration and attention on man and his economy. Stand still, and see the salvation of the Lord.

Though abundance comes through giving, a lot of people miss the opportunity and press toward the receiving end. I have found through my young walk in life that people address and accept you by what you can give to them. Maybe I'm a little shy of this area, but I've found that as long as you're constantly giving people your time, energy, or money, they Love you to death. But the moment this type of giving ceases, they seem to forget that you exist. I have learned that the strongest thing you can give these days are encouraging words and prayer. You see, prayer doesn't have a price tag attached. Once you've learned the earnestness and the reward of giving your time to God in prayer on behalf of others, He will reward you. I've come to an ultimate decision to stop trying to pacify others through monetary gifts and to give the gift of Love instead. That's pretty much all I can offer at this time. When God blesses me financially, I give. Most of the time, I find myself giving people even up to the last of what I have monetarily, but in the end it's still not enough. I am lead by the Spirit to give to others, but I don't make it a personal point; I make it a Godly point. He's the one who guides me into giving to others, and the blessings are manifested through him. "Give, and it shall be given unto you; good measures, pressed down, and shaken together, and running over, shall men give into your bosom. For with the same measure that ye mete withal it shall be measured t you again" (Luke 6:38).

By giving tithes and offerings, I open up another way for God to bless me. I give back to Him, and He blesses me. At first, I found it hard to give to Him first, but now I find it an ultimate relief because it all belongs to Him anyway. The challenge in life today is that people seem to put a price tag on everything, and if you don't hold up to your end monetarily, then you are cast out. People do not know your circumstances and situations, but they seem to follow the pattern of wondering what you are doing, how you are doing it, and why you are doing it, even when they do not know what is going on with you. It is a difficult, but promising, task to live strictly for God and not to lean towards man. Man will fail you, but God has the reward of blessing you. This is why He is my "All in All." I cannot live without His Love. Who is man that he will Love you so?

**B. Is My Blessing Others in Vain?**

I used to think that it was a cultural thing with people accepting you and loving you, but its people in general. Man has no place for you unless you are blessing Him in some way or another. This does not apply to everyone. For example, a few years ago, I had a long conversation with a brother who had recently ended a long-term relationship with a female who has three older children. Well, the relationship ended with an altercation between Him and one of her sons. It was a bitter situation I am sure, but it had to come to an end. Well, He in turn has three children himself. His biggest thing in our conversation is that life is just beginning for Him because His youngest child was about to graduate from high school. He can give advice and not be obligated to do anything else. Well, He introduced me to another female friend the night prior to this conversation and He was informing me of the history behind their relationship/friendship.

They had a relationship three years ago and they traveled while He was with the (other) long-term woman. The new female was in and out of relationships throughout this process, but now that His long-term relationship has ended she wanted to become a part of His current world. His biggest problem is that she has young children. He was adamant about not raising and contributing to someone else's children. His biggest argument was that whoever came to the table must come offering something. They had to give up something and be able to meet Him halfway. So much for Love, instead it had to be a business relationship. I had a problem with this because it was obvious that he misled the young lady into thinking that there would be something between them while he was still in a long-term relationship with someone else. The problem was that he was leading her on into thinking that they would establish their own relationship and that it would be unified and concrete. After a long discussion, I finally realized that it wasn't about loyalty, love, relationship, closeness, or anything that's genuine, but it was about bringing something to the table and offering nothing much in return.

This relates so much to giving because if we don't have Christ in our lives as our vital being than who can we expect to lean on? Somebody has to be real. People are not real and genuine anymore. I see it so often and as plain as day now because they want, and want and want but do not give anything in return. I've found that people think that you have a lot to give and they want it from you. It's not what I can do for you and yours, but what you can give to me and mine. This is a challenging situation and I see it more often than most. Some people don't care about you as an individual. They just want to know what you can give, what you got, and how they can acquire it from you. Even while my spouse was in Iraq, I really learned people as a whole. It was a few people who did something for the girls or me. The very ones He and I helped, assisted, and did a lot for in the past were the main ones I heard lip service but never got any results. Love is an action word. I should not have to ask for assistance, it should come naturally out of Love. It was a painful process to see how people, the very ones you think care really don't but I learned through it all to hold on to Jesus' everlasting arms and His Love. He was the only person real to me and truly cared. I have found that He will stay closer than any brother or friend. When you find a true friend, embrace them for who they really are in Christ.

You quickly learn who really cares for you when you are going through trials and tribulations. People are so wrapped up into their own world that they do not have time for you. It is when they want to find out what you are doing and how you are doing it when they become concerned about you. In the end, they do not care. That is why you must stay in prayer, seek the Lord with all of your heart and soul and see the flourishing that God has to offer. Forget about men and allow God to lead the way. He will tell you who to give to, why and how. Even when you find yourself giving and do not have a dime, seek the Lord. He will be your guide. He will never leave you nor forsake you. Let Him validate you, not man. Let Him be your all-in-all. "Let your conversation be without covetousness; and be content with such things as ye have: for He hath said, I WILL NEVER LEAVE THEE, NOR FORSAKE THEE. So that we may boldly say, THE LORD IS MY HELPER, AND I WILL NOT FEAR WHAT MAN SHALL DO UNTO ME" (Hebrews 13:5, 6).

Do not place your heart on the worldly possessions and on what the evil and ungodly people are obtaining but concentrate and keep your mind stayed on Jesus. He is placing everything in the Book of Remembrance. The proud and haughty may seem to be blessed, tempting God and going free; but the things we think, do, and say are recorded and God has a way of bringing it all back to our remembrance. "Blessed is that man that maketh the Lord His trust, and respecteth not the proud, nor such as turn aside to lies" (Psalm 40:4). During the Day of Judgment, I would rather hear the Lord say, "Well done good and faithful servant; enter, and I'll give you rest," as opposed to hearing Him ask me where my heart was, and for what reason was I blaspheming His noble name by not living according to the Word. Pray for a spirit of discernment to know the wicked and evil from the righteous. You don't have to accompany them but beware and do well, that's the Lord's request. Live only to please God and be obedient to His will. "But strong meat belongeth to them that are of full age, even those who by reason of use have their senses exercised to discern both good and evil" (Hebrews 5:14).

**Discussion Questions:**

1. **Have you robbed God?**

2. **What are some ways that can be identified as robbing God?**

3. **What will it profit a man to gain the world (monetarily) and lose his soul?**

4. **Is it worth it to have material gain out of the will of God?**

5. **Does God necessarily fulfill our needs materially?**

6. **Are tithes and offerings only monetary? Find it in scripture.**

7. **What will God say about you on Judgment Day?**

8. **Does giving always have to be monetary?**

**9. Is it challenging to give of yourself and your time?**

**10. When you bless others, is it in vain?**

**11. Have you found people who are truly concerned about you?**

**12. How do you handle those only interested in knowing your business, but they are not truly concerned about you?**

**Points to Discuss: After reading the lesson, go back and answer the questions in the lesson for an in-depth discussion.**

**Notes:**

## LESSON 21

# *Empower the People With a Word From God*

**Foundation: Exodus 4:10-16; 27-31**

*"And Moses said unto the Lord, O my Lord, I am not eloquent, neither heretofore, nor since Thou hast spoken unto Thy servant: but I am slow of speech, and of a slow tongue. And the Lord said unto him, 'Who hath made man's mouth? Or who maketh the dumb, or deaf, or the seeing, or the blind? Have not I the Lord? Now therefore go, and I will be with thy mouth, and teach thee what thou shalt say.' And he said, 'O my Lord, send, I pray Thee, by the hand of him whom thou wilt send.' And the anger of the Lord was kindled against Moses, and He said, 'Is not Aaron the Levite thy brother? I know that he can speak well. And also, behold, he cometh forth to meet thee: and when he seeth thee, he will be glad in his heart. And thou shalt speak unto him, and put words in his mouth: and I will be with thy mouth, and with his mouth, and will teach you what ye shall do. And he shall be thy spokesman unto the people: and he shall be, even he shall be to thee instead of a mouth, and thou shalt be to him instead of God.' And the Lord said to Aaron, 'Go into the wilderness to meet Moses.' And he went, and met him in the mount of God, and kissed him. And Moses told Aaron all the words of the Lord who had sent him, and all the signs which He had commanded him. And Moses and Aaron went and gathered together all the elders of the children of Israel: And Aaron spake all the words which the Lord had spoken unto Moses, and did the signs in the sight of the people. And the people believed: and when they heard that the Lord*

*had visited the children of Israel, and that He had looked upon their affliction, then they bowed their heads and worshiped."*

**A. Ignore Their Countenances**

Regardless of how you feel about speaking and telling people what thus sayeth the Lord, and regardless of what people say or feel, the main task for you to do is to speak a word. God can and will use anyone to tell people what He wants them to hear. He has told us in His Word that despite the countenance of their faces, and despite what they think or say, you just say the words that He gives you to speak."Thou therefore gird up thy loins, and arise, and speak unto them all that I command thee: be not dismayed at their faces, lest I confound thee before them" (Jeremiah 1:17). God is seeking bold and upright people to speak for Him. If you're reluctant to speak for God because you are looking at their faces and wondering what they are thinking or saying, then you will not be able to be used by God. The most important thing that He wants is for you to speak according to His word and not yours. You can't be a leader for Christ unless you're willing to bow down before Him. You must be at the point of belief and willingness in order to get to the level He would have you. There are situations you will face in life in order to meet His qualifications and requirements. You must be willing to go and speak whatever He deems. God is a loving God, and He's worthy to be praised. He's an awesome God who deserves true worship through our obedience to speak on His behalf. However, be wary; if you are not speaking a word from God, keep silent. "Now therefore go, and I will be with thy mouth, and teach thee what thou shalt say" (Exodus 4:12). Do not be hasty to say things that are not of God. Be mindful of what you say and do because people are always watching just to hear what you have to say, only to use it against you at an opportune time.

**B. Diligent Speakers Are Diligent Readers**

You cannot be bold to speak out for God if you are not aware of His Word. Be a diligent reader of His word, and stay in His face with prayer and supplication, knowing what He has in store for you. "Praying always with all prayer and supplication in the Spirit, and watching thereunto with all perseverance and supplication for all saints; and for me, that utterance may be given unto me, that I may open my mouth boldly, to make known the mystery of the gospel" (Ephesians 6:18, 19). The spoken word of God is best discerned when are aware of the written Word of God. Those who claim to speak for God, yet contradict what is written in His Word, are only fooling themselves and others. 2 Timothy 2:15 says, "Study to shew thyself approved unto God, a workman that needeth not be ashamed, rightly dividing the word of truth." When we read God's Word, we correctly discern the Spirit of the Lord when He gives us a word to speak.

God only wants to use you for His glory. Let Him have His way with your life. He'll be closer than any brother or friend. Let Him use you. Open your mouth and speak a word from the Lord. They want to hear from Him, and you have just what God has ordered. Speak and they will know that you've been in the presence of the Lord.

**Discussion Questions:**

1. **Are you speaking on God's behalf or on your own?**

2. **Do you see the need to speak on behalf of Christ in a dying and lost world?**

3. **Are you a leader for and follower of Christ?**

4. **Have you ever been convicted by the words you've spoken to someone?**

5. **Are you a diligent reader of the word?**

6. **Do you put what you read into practice?**

**Points to Discuss: After reading the lesson, go back and answer the questions in the lesson for an in-depth discussion.**

**Notes**

# LESSON 22

# Friends Bringing Friends for Healing

**Foundation: Luke 5:17-26**

*"And it came to pass on a certain day, as He was teaching, that there were Pharisees and doctors of the law sitting by, which were come out of every town of Galilee, and Judea, and Jerusalem: and the power of the Lord was present to heal them. And, behold, men brought in a bed a man which was taken with a palsy; and they sought means to bring him in, and to lay him before Him. And when they could not find by what way they might bring him in because of the multitude, they went upon the housetop, and let him down through the tiling with his couch into the midst before Jesus. And when He saw their faith, He said unto him, 'Man, thy sins are forgiven thee'. And the scribes and the Pharisees began to reason, saying, 'Who is this which speaketh blasphemies? Who can forgive sins, but God alone'? But when Jesus perceived their thoughts, He answering said unto them, 'What reason ye in your hearts? Whether is easier, to say, "Thy sins be forgiven thee"; or to say, "Rise up and walk?" But that ye may know that the Son of Man hath power upon earth to forgive sins,' (He said unto the sick of the palsy,) 'I say unto thee, arise, and take up thy couch, and go into thine house.' And immediately he rose up before them, and took up that whereon he lay, and departed to his own house, glorifying God. And they were all amazed, and they glorified God, and were filled with fear; saying, 'We have seen strange things today.'"*

Sometimes you may need someone to be there for you when you're healed. Just as the men lowered the paralyzed man through the rooftop to be healed by Jesus, we should do the same unto those whom we love. There are times when things may seem impossible and difficult, but know that there's nothing too hard for God. God allows situations and circumstances to take place in our lives for a reason. You see, if we strive on being obedient, cautious, and willing to believe and accept the things that God has in store for us, then we should understand that Christ can do all things but fail. We must place ourselves in God's controlling hands and fear Him with our lives. Nothing is too hard and impossible for him that believes. That is why it is imperative for us to have faith. We must have and keep a strong relationship with the Almighty. Jesus said it Himself: "But that ye may know that the Son of Man hath power on earth to forgive sins, then saith he to the sick of the palsy, 'Arise, take up thy bed, and go unto thine house'" (Matthew 9:6).

We must establish a right and prestigious relationship with God, look at our circumstances, and live for Jesus. No greater Love I know, than with the sweet and powerful name of Jesus. There is nothing too hard for God, if only we would just believe and receive it. When you have a friend who can be there with you through thick and thin, then you have a true friend. Times will get hard for everyone. We all have days in season and out of season. When experiencing difficult situations and going through trying times, lean and depend on God more so than man. Sometimes people can hear you and understand where you're coming from, but when they cannot seem to get the full revelation of what you're going through, lean on the Lord. He knows your heart and what you can bear more than anything or anyone. There are relationships in which friends are closer than family members. Relatives can become so familiar with who you once were that they fail to see who you can become. Friends, however, do not know the old you, with all of your stories and baggage, so they are more apt to hear you and understand the inner thoughts you are trying to convey and explain. Family are more apt to judge and to condemn you since they feel like you will never change and will always be that dramatic or deceitful person that you are or that you once were, but God knows the true person. He is developing you into the person who will truly worship and cling to Him.

True friends will be honest with you because that is all they know. Regardless of how hurtful they may seem, they are just being real. "Faithful are the wounds of a friend; but the kisses of an enemy are deceitful" (Proverbs 27:6). People don't appreciate someone who's real, they view it as negative. There are pessimistic people who view everything as something negative, but there are genuine people too. Genuine people are the ones you do not want to have a. relationship with due to the fear of having your feelings hurt. You feel they don't understand you and are just jealous of you. Before you write off genuine friends, try the spirit by the spirit to see if their words are true or not. "BELOVED, believe not every spirit, but try the spirits whether they are of God: because many false prophets are gone out into the world" (1 John 4:1).

**Discussion Questions:**

1. **Why do you think God allows things to be difficult and hard in life?**

2. **Why is it that some things are too hard for you but not God?**

3. **Do you have a strong relationship with God? Why or why not?**

4. **Are you closer to friends or family? Why?**

5. **Do you feel like you are a good, true friend where someone can depend on you?**

6. **Do your friends know your inner thoughts and the true you?**

7. **When you hear someone telling the truth do you feel they are negative or truthful?**

**Points to Discuss: After reading the lesson, go back and answer the questions in the lesson for an in-depth discussion.**

**Notes:**

## LESSON 23

# *Cleansing*

**Foundation: Luke 17:11-19; Philippians 4:6, 7**

*"And it came to pass, as He went to Jerusalem that He passed through the midst of Samaria and Galilee. And as He entered into a certain village, there met Him ten men that were lepers, which stood afar off. And they lifted up their voices, and said, 'Jesus, Master, have mercy on us.' And when He saw them, He said unto them, 'Go show yourselves unto the priests.' And it came to pass, that, as they went, they were cleansed. And one of them, when he saw that he was healed, turned back, and with a loud voice glorified God. And fell down on his face at His feet, giving Him thanks: and he was a Samaritan. And Jesus answering said, 'Were there not ten cleansed? But where are the nine? There are not found that returned to give glory to God, save this stranger.' And He said unto him, 'Arise, go thy way, thy faith hath made thee whole'" (Luke 17: 11-19).*

*"Be careful for nothing; but in everything by prayer and supplication with thanksgiving let your requests be made known unto God. And the peace of God, which passeth all understanding, shall keep your hearts and minds through Christ Jesus" (Philippians 4:6, 7).*

### A. From the Inside Out

Sometimes we can get caught up in being talkative and opinionated about others without recognizing that we are using idle words. It is imperative to constantly have a cleansing of the spirit on a daily basis. Recently, a fellow saint and I had a discussion about discernment, cliques, situations, such as power struggles, going on in churches with other saints, and rumors. I began to tell her that when certain people speak, text me and inform me so that I do not show up. Well of course this was a joke, but the more I thought about it later, the more convicted I became. We must be careful of the choice words we speak because they can come back to haunt us, even when you are joking, having fun, or just plain running your mouth. "But I say unto you, that every idle word that men shall speak, they shall give account thereof in the Day of Judgment" (Matthew 12:36). God has a purpose and plan for all of us. But we must tap into it with sincerity and run with it. Just as Jesus prayed and released others from infirmities, He can and will do the same for you. Just from that conversation alone I have learned and asked God to heal me from trying to change circumstances and situations and learn to adjust to it. I cannot change you and you cannot change me, but God is able to do exceedingly and abundantly above all that we can ever ask or think.

### B. Live and Let Live (Drop Your Burdens)

I have found myself getting too wrapped up and carved up into people's situations. Instead of just looking at the issue, staying on the outside of it, and praying that God make a way, I would become a part of the problem by trying to rectify and solve it myself from the inside when it did not concern me. From these situations, I have learned to live and let live. Even though I care, I still had to learn to distance myself from situations and not to let it consume me. Just as the ten lepers were healed when they left Jesus, I have been healed from carnality: too involved with other people's problems and too concerned with things that don't have any dealings with me. It is a disease, because the more I look at it, the more I see me, me, and me. God wants us to cast our cares on Him for He cares for us; however, we must leave it there. When people bring matters to my attention, my job is to pray and to leave it there, not to get wrapped up so tight that it becomes my own. Of course, I do not mean any harm when I show my concern; I just want to help rectify the problem. My main task in life has always been problem-solving, even from childhood; so, this is not nosiness, craziness, or haughtiness. It is just a concerned person who takes it to the next level and tries to reason and pray, but then tries to fix the problem herself. Some things cannot be fixed by human means. We must learn to fast, to pray, and to seek God on situations that are beyond our control. "AND He spake a parable unto them to this end, that men ought always to pray, and not to faint" (Luke 18:1).

### C. Be Kingdom-Minded

God has to remedy and change things around for all of us. We must learn to be Kingdom minded, not stuck on religion and people. In order to have a Kingdom mentality, you must be willing to step out of the realm of yourself and seek God in all things, especially those that are beyond your control. Be cleansed from the leper of control. Do not become a part of the problem, but give the problem to Jesus and live. I had to learn that all situations cannot be solved by me. I learned to let God have His way and to be at peace, to abound, and to be content in whatever state I am in. "Not that I speak in respect of want: for I have learned, in whatsoever state I am, therewith to be content" (Philippians 4:11).

The funny thing is that I was doing this outwardly, but inwardly, I was thinking of ways to help a situation that was spinning out of control. When people brought their problems, situations and circumstances to me, I constantly stayed in prayer for them. At the same time, I was trying to figure out a way to fix it. My task was to pray, to leave it with God, and to know that He would make a way somehow. I just wanted to have enough wisdom to know when something should and could be done to help the situation without becoming too involved. I was the leper in this situation because I was taking it upon myself to make it right, when ultimately God has all of the answers. I believe that God will show us solutions – how they can be executed and when is the right time to do it. The problem is knowing the "when." Do you respond immediately, after a while, or do you simply keep talking about it? No! Just pray, and God will tell you what to do. Leave it there. "Casting all your care upon him, for He careth for you" (1 Peter 5:7). As you wait on the Lord, keep people encouraged through Christ.

I have a habit of asking people if there is anything I can do to help them, if there is something they need for me to do or give, or if I'm allowed to have a conversation with them or others. This may be other people's normal ways of doing things, but for me, the thing that concerns me most is that I'm in the will of God. I don't want to overstep my boundaries with people and situations because all of these battles are not mine, they are the Lord's. "And He said, Hearken ye, all Judah, and ye inhabitants of Jerusalem, and thou king Jehoshaphat, Thus saith the Lord unto you, Be not afraid nor dismayed by reason of this great multitude; for the battle is not yours, but God's" (2 Chronicles 20:15). My prayer and concentration is for me to be in the will of and in tune with Christ at all times, whether I'm at church, home, work, or just around people. I have a tendency to excuse myself often when I'm around a crowd because I don't like it when cliques are formed, or when people start gossiping and saying things they will regret – just being out right ugly. This is a habit that needs to be broken because God told me to be abased, to abound, and to be at peace with everyone, even when the situation is uncomfortable and unbearable. I must learn to stick with it and pray. That's a challenge, but it is one that must be accomplished. Learn to dissolve the situation by listening and praying and directing every comment back to God. Just as the one leper came back to praise and worship God, we must learn to be the One in the crowd who takes the initiative to be part of righteousness and not to contribute to the problem. "For whosoever shall do the will of God, the same is my brother, and my sister, and mother" (Mark 3:35).

**Prayer: Lord, I thank you for granting me peace that surpasses all understanding, for giving me direction, and for giving me guidance. I also thank you, Lord, for giving me the spirit of discernment and likelihood and for allowing me to be your prayer warrior. These are powerful tools that can be used only through You. I Love you, Lord. Continue to bless and to keep me. Use me as your instrument and keep me safe from all hurt, harm, and danger. Amen!**

**Discussion Questions:**

1. **From what do you need to be cleansed and delivered?**

2. **Do you have bad habits that need to be broken?**

3. **Do you live and let live or do you get caught up in others situations?**

4. **Do you find yourself comfortable in cliques and gossiping?**

5. **Is God pleased with cliques, gossiping, back-biting, and lying?**

6. **How do you dissolve such atmosphere when you're around it or do you join it?**

**Points to Discuss: After reading the lesson, go back and answer the questions in the lesson for an in-depth discussion.**

**Notes:**

# LESSON 24

# *Where is Your Faith?*

**Foundation: Romans 5:1-6**

*"Therefore being justified by faith, we have peace with God through our Lord Jesus Christ: by whom also we have access by faith into this grace wherein we stand, and rejoice in hope of the glory of God. And not only so, but we glory in tribulations also: knowing that tribulation worketh patience; and patience, experience; and experience, hope: and hope maketh not ashamed; because the love of God is shed abroad in our hearts by the Holy Ghost which is given unto us. For when we were yet without strength, in due time, Christ died for the ungodly."*

## A. Praise Interlude

As I sit and think about the goodness of Jesus and all He has done for me, my soul cries out, "Hallelujah, anyhow!" May the grace and mercy of Him proceed to carry out the wondrous things He's done for and through me. May His mercies shine and endure forevermore. We as Christians must be careful to think mildly of ourselves and more mightily of God. "For I say, through the grace given unto me, to every man that is among you, not to think of himself more highly than He ought to think; but to think soberly, according as God hath dealt to every man the measure of faith" (Romans 12:3). He has brought us out of dangers seen and unseen. He has taught us how to place our faith and trust in Him. If we trust Him, why are we still at ground zero with our dreams, goals, and ambitions? If we say we believe, why do we sit on our gifts that He has placed on the inside of us and wait for someone else to carry it out or to pull it out? "Wherefore He saith, WHEN HE ASCENDED UP ON HIGH, HE LED CAPTIVITY CAPTIVE, AND GAVE GIFTS UNTO MEN" (Ephesians 4:8). Why do we look at what other people are saying and doing but not tending to our own affairs? "And that ye study to be quiet, and to do your own business, and to work with your own hands, as we commanded you; that ye may walk honestly toward them that are without, and that ye may have lack of nothing" (1 Thessalonians 4:11, 12).

## B. Faith According to Man or to God?

If we are law abiding citizens according to the Word, why do we judge one another? Why are we always consumed about what others have or have accomplished for themselves? It is mind boggling and worrisome to see people so fretful of change and advancement in the Kingdom. Why do we sit in the place and dictate, judge, form an opinion about, or say what we think others should do and how they should be when we have never taken a look in the mirror at ourselves? Who are you to judge? Just because you pray in the open does not mean I am not praying in my closet. Just because I do not attend all of your prayer visuals and sleepovers does not mean I am not praying. Who are you to think you are higher in the Kingdom than me? "For if a man think himself to be something, when he is nothing, he deceiveth himself" (Galatians 6:3).

Time is of the essence, and it is time for us to be about our Father's business. Why are we still sitting in the church house being fed on Sunday, Monday, Tuesday, Wednesday, Thursday, and Friday nights, but we're not in the community telling people about Christ and sharing our testimony with them? Why do we allow our comfort zones to rule and not make others excited about Christ and what He has done for us, so they can try someone new – Jesus? Why are we always singing the same tune about how bad it is, but still we have not proceeded to do anything about it?

## C. Whose Faith Approval Are You Seeking?

Who are you to look down on others and judge their characters when you don't even know them? Stop being so critical of others, and get back to the real heart of the matter: Jesus. He is the ultimate I AM. He is the great and wonderful Counselor. He is our Prince of Peace. He is the beginning, the middle, and the end. Do you not know that if it had not been for the Lord who was on our side, we would be outcasts into the darkness, princesses and princes of darkness, of the unknown, and of spiritual wickedness? While we are sitting in our same circles, trying to figure it out, the others have gotten it and are gone. They are no longer seeking it; they know it, eat it, sleep it, and breathe it. Guess what? If we do not get with it, we will be left behind and still trying to figure it out. "God also bearing them witness, both with signs and wonders, and with divers miracles, and gifts of the Holy Ghost, according to His own will" (Hebrews 2:4)? Why are we still here waiting? Pursue your dreams and the outlook you have on life. Go for what God told you to accomplish. Step out on faith and God will see you through. "Nay, in all these things we are more than conquerors through Him that loved us" (Romans 8:37). Stand still, and see the salvation of the Lord, for which He has set for you to accomplish today. He is waiting for you to precede now; what are you waiting for? It is time to go and not to be idle in your well doing. In all you do, do it giving reverence to the grace of God. (Additional Reading: Romans 3:21-4:25)

**Discussion Questions:**

1. **Have you stepped out on faith and believed God for a miracle?**

2. **Do you believe God can do the impossible in your situation?**

3. **Do you really trust God with your finances, business deal, or purchasing a home?**

4. **Are you judgmental?**

5. **Do you observe the man in the mirror to see what changes need to be made for the better?**

6. **Do you feel like God is on your side?**

7. **Are you self-righteous and put others down because they are not where you are in Christ?**

**Points to Discuss: After reading the lesson, go back and answer the questions in the lesson for an in-depth discussion.**

**Notes:**

## LESSON 25

# *Support the Wisdom of God With Training*

**Foundation: Ecclesiastes 7:11-29**

*"Wisdom is good with an inheritance: and by it there is profit to them that see the sun. For wisdom is a defense, and money is a defense: but the excellency of knowledge is, that wisdom giveth life to them that have it. Consider the work of God: for who can make that straight, which He hath made crooked? In the day of prosperity be joyful, but in the day of adversity consider: God also hath set the one over against the other, to the end that man should find nothing after him. All things have I seen in the days of my vanity: there is a just man that perisheth in his righteousness, and there is a wicked man that prolongeth his life in his wickedness. Be not righteous over much; neither make thyself over wise: why shouldest thou destroy thyself? Be not over much wicked, neither be thou foolish: why shouldest thou die before thy time? It is good that thou shouldest take hold of this; yea, also from this withdraw not thine hand: for he that feareth God shall come forth of them all. Wisdom strengtheneth the wise more than ten mighty men which are in the city. For there is not a just man upon earth, that doeth good, and sinneth not. Also take no heed unto all words that are spoken; lest thou hear thy servant curse thee:*

*For oftentimes also thine own heart knoweth that thou thyself likewise hast cursed others. All this have I proved by wisdom: I said, 'I will be wise,' but it was far from me. That which is far off, and exceeding deep, who can find it out? I applied mine heart to know, and to search, and to seek out wisdom, and the reason of things, and to know the wickedness of folly, even of foolishness and madness: And I find more bitter than death the woman, whose heart is snares and nets, and her hands as bands: whoso pleaseth God shall escape from her; but the sinner shall be taken by her. Behold, this have I found, saith the preacher, counting one by one, to find out the account: Which yet my soul seeketh, but I find not: one man among a thousand have I found; but a woman among all those have I not found. Lo, this only have I found, that God hath made man upright; but they have sought out many inventions".*

### A. Be "Wise as Serpents…."

As I ventured into the Word, I discovered that God made us in His own image and gave us knowledge to fulfill the desires and know-how of this world. We go on our tangents about education according to the world, but how are we to be knowledgeable if we have not tapped into the wisdom of God through His Word? God told us to be wise according to the time and to get knowledge and understanding. "For the LORD giveth wisdom: out of His mouth cometh knowledge and understanding" (Proverbs 2:6). If we are supposed to tap into our gifts, why is it a hassle or struggle for us to receive wisdom from those who have greater knowledge about our gifts than we do? There are circumstances and situations that seem right to us, but we are reluctant to try because of the messenger. This is bias on your behalf, but it is also challenging because now you are being judgmental. We are to test the fruit of the Spirit to know if they are of God or not, but instead we have tested and tried ourselves to see what it is we are to master.

There is not a problem with having the natural know-how in a certain field and, at the same time, being able to get more wisdom from someone else who knows better and can impart their knowledge into you to help you master your area of expertise. God says we have not because we ask not, but are we asking for earthly wisdom? Are we asking for the know-how according to the world? Are we seeking God for direction and better understanding of the things we see and know? Have we dipped into the inner challenges to see where we can be rectified and still know that God is in control? Have we examined our whole self to see if we are true examples of the living God? Do we see and know that God is in full control of this world, even Man's so-called system? It is time we get a grip to understand that God has filled us with wisdom, but it is up to us to tap into the inner knowledge where we can master it and better ourselves for the next level for which God is equipping us to go.

## B. Ask the Divine Expert What to Do

Why are we idle and sitting, waiting for hand-me-downs but jealous about someone else's blessings? Why are we constantly watching and hating others for their accomplishments but too scared to get our own? Why are we always discussing somebody else's business when we need to be focused on what God has called us to do? Why do we run away from knowledge when it only comes to make us better people and more in the know, which is beneficial, according to God's Word and, believe it or not, to man? Why not acquire more knowledge to know how to make it in life? Why not expand yourself to even greater heights to see where the Lord will take you? God created us to be doctors, lawyers, nurses, teachers, preachers, managers, sales clerks, judges, secretaries, and janitors; all of us were made in His image. Isn't it good for doctors to attend college and to become a master in their expertise? If they did not they wouldn't be able to perform miracles (according to the Lord) with our health. God is able to use the education of the world to help us in what He has called us to do. He is able to cause the system of the world to advance us in His holy calling. So why do we struggle with education according to man's system? Why do we question and put those "educated people" down who have made something out of themselves, only to better themselves and to be able to make it.

We get tired of church folks coming to church to beg for handouts, but oftentimes, these are the ones without the skills or the know-how to get ahead. We complain that they should go back to school or get experience in something beneficial, but at the same time, we overlook that it is man's system, a technical college or a place of higher learning, where they will acquire the "know." It seems like we got it twisted. Sometimes we become so religious and into ourselves that we forget that God gave man dominion over the earth to men–to subdue it. The Word of God tells us to be "in the world but not of the world" (Romans 12:2). People of God are able to get the know-how and skills they need to get ahead without sacrificing their faith in the Most High.

## C. Do You Know the Wisdom and Plan That God Has for You?

During the process of all of this, we are tested to be obedient children who focus on the gifts and charities of God and who venture out into His realm of life. He granted it to us that we might fulfill the desires of our hearts and accomplish the goals and dreams we set out to do. Why do we remain idle, complaining and wondering? Why not just go do it? Find your know-how, or desire, and go for what God has placed on the inside of you. It is your dream or desire. It is what you know best from God. Seek God, and do well. You can still be saved, sanctified, and filled with the Holy Ghost. You will just master it with a seal. Yes, that piece of paper tells man what you know and can do, but God has even greater plans for you. Just test Him, try Him, and see that He is God, and that He shall not lie. He has a plan even greater for you. If your desire is to counsel, then counsel but support your work with some form of training or documentation to speak for you. Whatever you desire, whatever you strive for and plan in life, just seek the Lord, and He will be there to see you through. When we go through trials and tribulations, it is the testing of our faith that makes us stronger, but it is more so the zeal and desire of God that carries us through to reach our vital point in life. Check yourself and see what your true fruit really shows. Yes, there are people in the world who know a whole lot more than we do; we just have to tap into it and find out. "Even so faith, if it hath not works, is dead, being alone" (James 2:17). Where is your faith? Are you caught up on religion and holiness to the point where you cannot get any training from anyone to better yourself because they are not Godly enough for you? Sometimes we are our own enemy and we get too caught up into our own self- righteousness and forget that we are spirits enclosed in a fleshly body. It is our spirit that consumes God and man, but it is the body that operates in the mechanics of things. Be holy and knowledgeable to God. (Additional Reading: Ecclesiastes 8, 9)

**Discussion Questions:**

1. **Are you self-righteous and put others down because they are not where you are in Christ? Does this keep you from receiving the Word of the Lord from them?**

2. **Have you tapped into and are exercising your gift(s) from God?**

3. **Are you reluctant to try your gift because someone prophesied, or did not prophesy, to you about it?**

4. **Are you using your gift to the glory of God or for your own glory?**

5. **What is your fruit? Has your fruit been hindered by not pursuing further learning, i.e. education or training?**

6. **What do you have to offer for Christ with your fruits?**

7. **Do you ever lift someone else up to aid them in being better for Christ?**

8. **Do you challenge others with gifts in going forth for Christ?**

**Points to Discuss: After reading the lesson, go back and answer the questions in the lesson for an in-depth discussion.**

**Notes:**

## LESSON 26

# *The Spirit and Righteousness of God*

**Foundation: 2 Corinthians 5:16-21; Proverbs 8:13;
Galatians 5:25-26; 6:3; Matthew 6:5**

*"Wherefore henceforth know we no man after the flesh; yea, though we have known Christ after the flesh, yet now henceforth know we Him no more. Therefore if any man be in Christ, he is a new creature: old things are passed away; behold, all things are become new. And all things are of God, who hath reconciled us to Himself by Jesus Christ, and hath given to us the ministry of reconciliation: to wit, that God was in Christ, reconciling the world unto Himself, not imputing their trespasses unto them; and hath committed unto us the word of reconciliation. Now then we are ambassadors for Christ, as though God did beseech you by us: we pray you in Christ's stead, be ye reconciled to God. For He hath made Him to be sin for us, who knew no sin; that we might be made the righteousness of God in him" (2 Corinthians 5:16-21).*

*"If we live in the Spirit, let us also walk in the Spirit. Let us not be desirous of vain glory, provoking one another, envying one another" (Galatians 5:25, 26).*

*"For if a man think himself to be something, when he is nothing, he deceiveth himself" (Galatians 6:3).*

*"The fear of the Lord is to hate evil: pride, and arrogancy, and the evil way, and the froward mouth, do I hate" (Proverbs 8:13).*

*"And when thou prayest, thou shall not be as the hypocrites are: for they love to pray standing in the synagogues and in the corners of the streets, that they may be seen of men. Verily I say unto you, they have their reward" (Matthew 6:5).*

### A. Who Are You Deceiving?

There are times when people think of themselves more highly than they ought. They seem to get carried away with pride and righteousness and thinking that they're better than others because of what they have materially and not about the magnitude of God. There are the self-righteous who are called the religious sanctified saints who think that because they outwardly pray they are more blessed and highly favored than the next person. There are some who feel that no one or only certain people are worthy to acquaint themselves with them and that others are forbidden. They do not allow others to visit their home, and they cannot be around those they deem "unworthy"; if they are, they treat them with very little discourse and are distant from that person, as not to be bothered. But God is the ultimate Judge. He sees all and knows all. He is the Creator; He is our all in all. If He allowed people, who were not holy, to surround Him–people who were sinners, wine bibbers, and gangsters–then who are we to shut off ourselves from those who delight themselves in the presence of the Lord? God says to humble ourselves in His sight and allow Him to use us to which we are His vessels and anointed ones. "For whosoever exalteth himself shall be abased; and He that humbleth himself shall be exalted" (Luke 14:11).

When people see you, they should see Christ. If you are so holy, why do you not give the beggar the time of day? Why do you not entertain strangers? Why do you not allow those who are mischievous to come into your presence and give them a word from God? Why do you think you are better and higher than a fellow saint who you see regularly? Why do you walk around and talk badly about people who have trusted you with their innermost thoughts and care while you belittle them to your clique or fellow gossipers? Does everyone but you have something wrong with them? It's funny that only the ones who bow down to your sanctimonious jokes and conversations can relate to your world, only those who shout and scream to be seen can enter into your court. That's a dangerous concept.

### B. Have You Been in His Presence?

Sometimes we need to slip into the council of the Most High and ask Him to renew our minds and thought processes. We need to get Him to strip us and let us know who we really are in His sight. We need to do self-examination and see our faults and actions. Even when we think we are holier than others, in His presence we see that we are no better than the next person. We must allow the Holy Spirit to fully reign, rule, and govern our walk with Christ to make sure we are obedient and in the will of God. What kind of spirit is dwelling in you and through you? Who are you with your "wanna be" pious self? When was the last time you took off your mask and allowed God to tell you who you really are behind the scenes of life? Who are you to judge and talk down on and about others? Get your own house in order before you go out talking about what the churches and people have not done for you. What are you doing within your walls and for yourself? Are you reading and living the Word? Are you praying? Are you truly seeking God to know who you really are as a person?

Are you continuing to wear the mask and pretend to be someone you are not? How can you judge anybody when you have not done a self-inventory? How can you put your mouth on the man and woman of God and their children when your house and family here and afar are in outrage, doing what they want, and living any kind of way? Who are you to judge and make false accusations about people who you really do not know, only what they tell you, but you do not know them for yourself? When was the last time you truly sought to help someone else outside of your circle? When was the last time you gave a kind word to a fellow co-worker/colleague or church member? When was the last time you did something nice for someone else and not look for someone to bless you? When was the last time you went into your finances and aided with someone else's expense without seeking assistance from others yourself? When was the last time you truly sought the face of the Lord and asked, "What must I really do to be saved and live according to your word and will and not my own without a hidden agenda?"

### C. What Has God Said to You Lately?

Have you heard from the Lord about your circle? What did He say? Was He the One to give you your orders this time, or did someone else? Did you really take a long clear look in the mirror to see yourself? What are you doing that is so righteous that you think you are better than everybody else? You must get on and stay on your face; do a holy self-evaluation, and ask God to clean you inside and out. Everyone should know without a shadow of a doubt that you are a child of the Most High. If not, check yourself through God's eyes. What is your passion in life? Do you seek after God for directions, leadership, and guidance or do you make your own decisions? Guess what? It is not about you. It is about the direction and leading of God. Seek God for the things you desire to do and be and let Him manifest Himself through you to make it happen. Why do we drain ourselves looking for material gain and wealth when we can look to the hills from which cometh our help (Psalm 121:1, 2)? Let Him prove and show Himself faithful in the midst of it all. Do you ever wonder why you are not as wealthy as you think you should be or why you do not have the things you truly desire? Do you feel as though your desires are eluding you? Has God spoken a word to you regarding the secrets of your heart? If you would seek God and look for His guidance, He will give you the desires of your heart. Have you been wondering why some requests seem to have been left unanswered. Maybe you are not spiritually ready. Maybe you have not sought Him wholly for what He desires for your life. Maybe you need to regroup and understand that the things you're seeking after are not really in your best interest. Maybe you are not to have material wealth, but spiritual wealth. "Beloved, I wish above all things that thou mayest prosper and be in health, even as thy soul prospereth" (3 John 2).

Sometimes we need to understand that there is a light at the end of the tunnel, but we are not ready to be used by God to handle the material wealth. Are you willing to give away everything you possess to follow God? Are you ready to give up friends and family to do the will of God? Are you ready to turn loose bad habits and to seek God's face for the true wealth of His Kingdom? Are you ready to reach down into the lowest of the low to talk to someone and show them how to live righteously for God? Are you ready to come out of yourself and be who God would have you to be for Him so that He can work in and through you? Are you ready to surrender your whole self to Him? "For I rejoiced greatly, when the brethren came and testified of the truth that is in thee, even as thou walkest in the truth. I have no greater joy than to hear that my children walk in truth" (3 John 3, 4). If you are ready and are able to be kind and affectionate to your enemy, then you may be ready to do the true will of the Father. Seek God for guidance and understanding, and He will see you through.

**Discussion Questions:**

1. **What does it mean to walk in the Spirit?**

2. **How do you die daily to the flesh?**

3. **Why do you invite yourself to others' homes but refuse to allow them in your home?**

4. **Are you too sanctimonious for Christ?**

5. **Do you feel that you're better than others when they are going through difficult times?**

6. **Are you passionate enough to lead others to Christ without changing who they are so that they mimic your deceitful ways?**

7. **Are you living for your own selfish gain having others follow you or are you truly leading them to Christ?**

8. **Are you seeking your own desires and not that of God's?**

**Points to Discuss: After reading the lesson, go back and answer the questions in the lesson for an in-depth discussion.**

**Notes:**

# LESSON 27

# Where Are You Spiritually When Jesus Heals You?

**Foundation: Luke 17:11-19**

*"And it came to pass, as He went to Jerusalem that He passed through the midst of Samaria and Galilee. And as He entered into a certain village, there met Him ten men that were lepers, which stood afar off. And they lifted up their voices, and said, Jesus, Master, have mercy on us. And when He saw them, He said unto them, 'Go show yourselves unto the priests.' And it came to pass, that, as they went, they were cleansed. And one of them, when He saw that He was healed, turned back, and with a loud voice glorified God, And fell down on His face at His feet, giving Him thanks; and He was a Samaritan. And Jesus answering said, 'Were there not ten cleansed? But where are the nine? There are not found that returned to give glory to God, save this stranger. And He said unto him, 'Arise, go thy way; thy faith hath made thee whole."*

## A. Locate Yourself

Where are you in the spirit when you've cried out year after year, pondering if God will heal you from this, that, and the other? When drug addicts are tired of being sick and tired, when prostitutes are tired of lying down with every Tom, Dick and Harry; when liars are tired of repulsive lying and trying to cover up one lie after the other; when crooks are tired of stealing and beating people out of their things? Where are you when God delivered you out of your mess and allowed you to get it together *again*? I say "again" because you messed up once before, before that, and again before that. Has it occurred to you that every aspect of our lives are spiritual journeys that we walk through and keep walking through over and over again. Are we aligned with God? Sometimes it doesn't take a rocket scientist to show us ourselves and our mess that we have gotten ourselves into from not giving God the thanks, the glory and the honor for keeping us all over again.

### B. Spiritual Growth in God

It is time to put down the bottle of milk and to chew on the meat of God's Word. It is time to dissect spiritual food for spiritual healing, once and for all. Why do we sit and ponder day after day about what we are doing with our lives? How are we going to make it? Where is God taking us now? Has it not occurred to you that God keeps giving us chance upon chance to get it together but that we have become our own enemies? We sit back and look at the lives of others, wishing for their success, but we never second guess the decisions that have turned our realities into a mess. I look at my own life as an example. God constantly put ideas and thoughts into my mind of things to do and that must be done to enlighten the Kingdom for His glorification, but until I lay aside my caution and sit there to analyze, to wonder, to dream, and to think, nothing will happen. If I keep sitting and sitting instead of moving, responding, and acting on faith on behalf of Christ, then I will always keep thinking and never stepping out on faith. Well, baby girl and baby boy, it is time to grow up; it is time to get it together. God did not give you multiple gifts just to sit there and sleep on them, talk about them, and wonder if He is really going to use them. No; He gave them to you so you could step out on faith and see the salvation of the Lord.

### C. Are You the Thankful Healed Leper?

Let me explain how we can become our own enemies. Sometimes, we can be like the nine lepers in Luke 17 who were ungrateful and did not think enough of Jesus to tell Him thank you for healing them." We tend to get arrogant and boastful because we think we've healed ourselves and lifted ourselves out of our mess. Life is funny, we all go through the ups, downs, and mishaps of life; we think we've pulled ourselves up "by our own bootstraps." Do we ever think about the goodness of Jesus and His miracles that we take so for granted every day? Nine of the 10 lepers kept going and never thanked God for healing and deliverance. It was only the stranger, the foreigner, the Samaritan. He was the only one who gave Jesus the glory and honor for his curing and relief. Even Jesus questioned this act of being unthankful, ungrateful, and unworthy gratitude from the Jews. They remind me of the people that Paul warned against in 1Timothy 1:6-10; 13-15; 2Timothy 3:1-9. These are the sick people in the spirit and in the sight of God.

**D. Are You Caught Up with Cliques or Christ?**

Earlier in the book, we talked about cliques. Let's revisit this topic. We get so caught up with being righteous to ourselves and our cliques that we forget the truth behind righteousness. We disdain other people to hang around because they are not saved enough, holy enough, righteous enough (in our own sight). You know it is at the point and time where the Lord is tired, the earth is tired of us and our mess, the world itself is trembling because we (with our righteous self) have made such a mess of things that God himself has to come down and get it right and Holy again. Adam and Eve messed it up from the beginning and ever since it has not been right. It is time to pick up the real meaning of life and put the bottle down so we can eat the meat and bread from Christ. God did not give us a spirit of fear, but of sound mind, but the transgression of the wicked saith within His heart, that there is no fear of God before His eyes (Psalm 36:1). Psalm 37 tells us to fret not the evil doer, trust in the Lord and do good. Delight thyself in the Lord and He shall give you the desires of your heart. It is time out eating and entangling in the wrong doings of this world. It is time to align ourselves with God and seek the greater rewards He has for our future.

**E. Do You Think Too Highly of Yourself?**

Why is it that we think more highly of ourselves than we ought? Why is it that we think we are better than Christ our Creator when we are nothing? Why it is that we often place our own needs over the needs of our brothers and sisters in Christ, as if no one else is better than we are? Search your heart, mind, body, and soul, and ask God to clean you of your leprosy. Go back and give God thanks, glory, and honor for acknowledging you. He did not have to do it, but He did. He did not forget you. He thought enough of you to get you where you are today, and He desires to take you higher, but you forgot about Him. You've gotten caught up in *yourself*, and you did not honor *Him*. So you dropped off God at the original point of your destination. He wants you to let His light shine in you so that men, women, boys and girls can see the salvation of the Lord in you, in your walk, in your talk, and in your being. God has not forgotten His words toward you; it is just that you forgot to thank and acknowledge Him. Go your way, and let the goodness of Jesus be manifested in and through you. He is waiting on you to put down the wondering and pondering to see His goodness and to step out on faith for His salvation and glory. Stop sleeping; stop talking; stop wondering; stop analyzing, and start doing something for the glory of the Lord! Don't be like the children of Israel who murmured against the Lord in Exodus 16:6-8. They thought they were murmuring against Moses and Aaron but they were actually murmuring against our Provider, the only one who can supply ALL of our needs according to His riches in glory. Amen! Amen! Amen!

**Discussion Questions:**

1. **Where are you? Do you have a relationship with Christ or are you tied up in the world?**

2. **Are you crying out to the Lord for direction and healing?**

3. **Are you aligned with Christ in the spirit?**

4. **Has God given you chance after chance to make it right, but you're still comfortable in your mess?**

5. **Do you bounce back after a failure and continue to fulfill the mission and walk for Christ, or do you go along for the ride hoping to change yourself eventually?**

6. **Do you take God for granted?**

7. **Does God really have to fulfill any miracles or healings for you?**

**8. Do you think more highly of yourself than you ought? Is God pleased with you?**

**Points to Discuss: After reading the lesson, go back and answer the questions in the lesson for an in-depth discussion.**

**Notes:**

# LESSON 28

# A Watchman for God's People

### Foundation: Ezekiel 3:17-27

*"Son of man, I have made thee a watchman unto the house of Israel: therefore hear the word at My mouth, and give them warning from Me. When I say unto the wicked, 'Thou shalt surely die'; and thou givest him not warning, nor speakest to warn the wicked from his wick way, to save his life; the same wicked man shall die in his iniquity; but his blood will I require at thine hand. Yet if thou warn the wicked, and he turn not from his wickedness, nor from his wicked way, he shall die in his iniquity; but thou hast delivered thy soul. Again, when a righteous man doth turn from his righteousness, and commit iniquity, and I lay a stumbling block before him, he shall die: because thou hast not given him warning, he shall die in his sin, and his righteousness which he hath done shall not be remembered; but his blood will I require at thine hand. Nevertheless if thou warn the righteous man, that the righteous sin not, and he doth not sin, he shall surely live, because he is warned; also thou hast delivered thy soul. And the hand of the Lord was there upon me; and he said unto me; 'Arise, go forth into the plain, and I will there talk with thee.' Then I arose, and went forth into the plain: and behold, the glory of the Lord stood there, as the glory which I saw by the river of Chebar: and I fell on my face. Then the spirit entered into me, and set me upon my feet, and spake with me, and said unto me, 'Go, shut thyself within thine house. But thou, O son of man, behold, they shall put bands upon thee, and shall bind thee with them, and thou shalt not go out among them: And I will make thy tongue cleave to the roof of thy mouth, that thou shalt be dumb, and shalt not be to them a reprover: for they are a rebellious house. But when I speak with thee, I will open thy mouth,*

*and thou shalt say unto them, "Thus saith the Lord God; he that heareth, let him hear; and he that forbeareth, let him forbear; for they are a rebellious house.""*

**A. Speak, O Watchman**

Tell them what thus sayeth the Lord. Like Ezekiel, go into the plain and God will speak with you there. Warn the wicked to turn from their wicked ways. Warn the righteous man who has turned from righteousness to turn back. If not, they will die in iniquity. Say to yourself, "If I don't tell or warn them, the blood will be on my hands." He will equip you with what you need to tell the people, but we must be sure to adhere to God's timing. "And I will make thy tongue cleave to the roof of thy mouth, that thou shalt be dumb, and shalt not be to them a reprover: for they are a rebellious house." (Ezekiel 3:26). Sometimes, we know that God has given us a word for the people, but it is not the appropriate time to speak. God's Word says that He will make your tongue stick to the roof of your mouth so that you cannot speak until the time is right. He will let you know when.

It is the season to be boisterous enough to say what thus saith the Lord to a dying world. People are mixed up and confused about so many things in life. Children do not have a voice in their identity. Teens do not have anyone with whom they can share their experiences because the parents are too busy entertaining others or climbing the corporate ladder. Babies are giving birth and raising babies. Everybody is busy doing something but doing nothing at the same time. At the end of the day will it matter if you have achieved a higher title with more workload and less interaction with your children? Will it matter if you are driving an expensive car and have no love in your home? Will it make a difference if you have money in your bank account and stocks with a high return but your home has no love or direction from God? We are nearing the end of this world. There are so many things happening in this world that show the definite signs of the end of time. God is raising up a nation to speak on His behalf to a dying world. He wants an Ezekiel to prophesy words of wisdom to His people. There are young people who desire to know what to expect in the last days. There are middle aged and older people who see the destruction of the world's system and who have a keen understanding that the world is coming to an end; however, they refuse to share it with the nations. With everything going on in the world, we see that we are in a rebellious time, but no one seems to take time to hear from the Lord. He is growing tired and anxious because of the destructions of this world. He is growing tired of our excuses. He is tired of us. Are you going to speak like Ezekiel or will He cleave your tongue to the roof of your mouth? Are you a watchman for Israel or are you a contributing part of a dying world?

### B. God Will Bring Judgment Against the Nations

"For men shall be lovers of their own selves, covetous, boasters, proud, blasphemers, disobedient to parents, unthankful, unholy. Without natural affection, trucebreakers, false accusers, incontinent, fierce, despisers of those that are good. Traitors, heady, high-minded, lovers of pleasures more than lovers of God; having a form of godliness, but denying the power thereof from such turn away. For of this sort are they which creep into houses, and lead captive silly women laden with sins, led way with diver's lusts. Ever learning, and never able to come to the knowledge of the truth. Now as Jannes and Jambres withstood Moses, so do these also resist the truth: men of corrupt minds, reprobate concerning the faith. But they shall proceed no further; for their folly shall be manifest unto all men, as theirs also was. But thou hast fully known my doctrine, manner of life, purpose, faith, long-suffering, charity, patience, Persecutions, afflictions, which came unto me at Antioch, at Iconium, at Lystra, what persecutions I endured: but out of them all the Lord delivered me. Yea, and all that will live godly in Christ Jesus shall suffer persecution. But evil men and seducers shall wax worse and worse, deceiving, and being deceived. But continue thou in the things which thou hast learned and hast been assured of, knowing of whom thou hast learned them. And that from a child thou hast known the holy scriptures which are able to make thee wise unto salvation through faith which is in Christ Jesus. All scripture is given by inspiration of God, and is profitable for doctrine, for reproof, for correction, for instruction in righteousness; That the man of God may be perfect, thoroughly furnished unto all good works" (2 Timothy 3:2-17).

The world is becoming so cunning and confusing. People are *choosing* if they want to be a male or a female instead of accepting God's gift of who they are. This world has turned into a crooked and perverse generation. God promised He would pour out His spirit among us. "And it shall come to pass afterward, that I will pour out My spirit upon all flesh; and your sons and your daughters shall prophesy; your old men shall dream dreams; your young men shall see visions" (Joel 2:28). This is when you will know that you have been in the presence of the Lord. God is waking up His army of men and women, preparing them to go on His battlefield. He's preparing the crooked way and making it straight. There are sons and daughters that were sold for their earthly parents' benefits to fulfill the lusts of their hearts. Greed, drunkenness, wine, sex, money, and lies are more important to them than being parents, but God is bringing up a generation that will go into the enemy's camp and take back what the devil has stolen from us. He is bringing up a nation who will not stammer or be in doubt because they know the God that we serve is more than enough; He is our Provider, our Healer, our Ruler, and the God of a second chance. He is raising up a nation that will be bold and not weary about telling people about the works of Christ.

**C. Can You Hear From God for the People?**

Stand still, and hear a word from God. If there are too many noises and distractions, go into your secret place, and hear from God. He has something to say. It is time for us to let the wicked know that they are wicked and that it's time to turn from their wicked ways. It is time for us to let the righteous man know that he cannot fail God. Either his heart is for Christ, or it is against Him. The righteous cannot hide from God. Are you going to church but still watching pornography? Are you lusting after people who don't belong to you and cheating on your spouse? Are you seeking after beer, wine, and drugs for a quick fix? Are you questioning your sex, wondering if you want to be a man or a woman? It is time to get it right. Either you will live for Him, or you will die in iniquity. Pull off the masks, air out your dirtiness, and seek God. Who are you fooling? This is the trickery of the enemy. "Love not the world, neither the things that are in the world. If any man love the world, the love of the Father is not in him. For all that is in the world, the lust of the flesh, and the lust of the eyes, and the pride of life, is not of the Father, but is of the world. And the world passeth away, and the lust thereof; but He that doeth the will of God abideth forever" (1 John 2:15-17).

Get with the Word, and let that be your guide. Seek God, and turn from wickedness and self righteousness. "Delight thyself also in the Lord; and He shall give thee the desires of thine heart" (Psalm 37:4). Where are the humble and the meek? The Bible tells us, "Blessed are the meek: for they shall inherit the earth" (Matthew 5:5). Everybody wants to be seen and heard but nobody seeks God. God said, "If My people, which are called by My name, shall humble themselves, and pray, and seek My face, and turn from their wicked ways; then will I hear from heaven, and will forgive their sin, and will heal their land" (2 Chronicles 7:14). Jesus commanded us to "go ye therefore, and teach all nations, baptizing them in the name of the Father; and of the Son, and of the Holy Ghost: teaching them to observe all things whatsoever I have commanded you: and, lo, I am with you always, even unto the end of the world. Amen" (Matthew 28:19-20). It is our duty "to open their eyes, and to turn them from darkness to light, and from the power of Satan unto God, that they may receive forgiveness of sins, and inheritance among them which are sanctified by faith that is in Me" (Acts 26:18). "But that which ye have already hold fast till I come. And he that overcometh, and keepeth My works unto the end, to Him will I give power over the nations" (Revelation 2:25-26). Seek Christ while you still have time.

## D. Are You Able to Pass the Test?

It is the time and season to speak because Christ is coming much sooner than we think. He is searching for a church, a body without spot or wrinkle. The Word tells us, "…that He might present it to Himself a glorious church, not having spot, or wrinkle, or any such thing; but that it should be holy and without blemish" (Ephesians 5:27). He is seeking those who will say, "For God, I will live; and for Him, I will die." Can you say, "My life is clean, and my house is in order?" How can I tell you what you need to do if junk is in my trunk? Clean the speck out of your own eye before you try to clean mine. Sweep around your own front door before you try to sweep around mine. There are people who are living lies and pretending they are sons and daughters of God, but their lives are a total wreck. How can you minister to someone else when you are in a mess yourself? Are you truly seeking God? Are you living the true life of God?

It is time to get your life in order. It is time to live it, sleep it, breathe it, acquire it, obtain it, feel it, and know it. Once you know who you are then you will know whose you are. Once you know whose you are, then you will be able to claim that you are a child of God. The war is on, and the men and women of God are coming out bolder than ever, just like Ezekiel. Are you ready to stand the test? Can you put your best foot forward? Are you ready to say, "For Him, I will live; and for Him, I will die?" Are you selling your birthright to the devil? Are you like Esau, who considered his inheritance worthless? As it says in the Bible, "…lest there be any fornicator, or profane person, as Esau, who for one morsel of meat sold his birthright. For ye know how that afterward, when he would have inherited the blessing, he was rejected: for he found no place of repentance, though he sought it carefully with tears" (Hebrews 12:16-17, see original scripture, Genesis 25:19-34).

## E. Are You Alienating Yourself from the World?

Are you alienating yourself from the world because of self-righteousness? You'd rather stand back and judge the world than go forth and help deliver it. Or perhaps the shame of hidden sins has caused you to forget who you are, and you've isolated yourself from others instead of repenting and moving forward. Maybe you're going through a hard time, and you've chosen to "hide out" until something happens. The Word of God gives us a different road; are you willing to believe that and behave as if nothing can separate you from the Love of God? "Who shall separate us from the love of Christ? Shall tribulation, or distress, or persecution, or famine, or nakedness, or peril, or sword" (Romans 8:35)? Are you ready to come out of yourself and truly go into the highways and byways to tell people about Christ? Are you ready to speak, knowing that some people may walk away, that some may bring your past back to judge, and that some may question your right to speak on His goodness? Can they look at your life, listen to you talk, and know that you truly are a child of God? Will they see Jesus in you? Don't fall for the schemes of the world. Be the true child of God whom you were meant to be. Let the world know that you truly have been in the presence of God!

Scripture tells us that Jesus told the disciples to go and share the good news about Him. He said, "A good man out of the good treasure of his heart bringeth forth that which is good; and an evil man out of the evil treasure of his heart bringeth forth that which is evil: for of the abundance of the heart his mouth speaketh" (Luke 6:45). Paul tells us in Colossians 4:2-6, "Continue in prayer, and watch in the same with thanksgiving." Withal praying also for us, that God would open unto us a door of utterance, to speak the mystery of Christ, for which I am also in bonds: that I may make it manifest, as I ought to speak. Walk in wisdom toward them that are without, redeeming the time. Let your speech be always with grace, seasoned with salt, that you may know how ye ought to answer every man." With whom are you sharing Christ today? Are you being a witness for Him? Are you letting your light shine, or is it hidden so far under a bushel that no one can see it? Are you ready to leave the "me" and "I" to pick up your cross and follow Jesus? Are you ready to go where He leads you, regardless of the situation or circumstances? Are you ready to "put on the whole armor of God, that ye may be able to stand against the wiles of the devil" (Ephesians 6:11)?

God is tired. He is seeking a church on fire for Him. He is seeking a church that does not mind serving Him, telling people about Him, and – in other words, "keeping it real." It is okay to be right with God. It is okay to *live* righteously. It is okay to tell a dying world that Jesus lives! Also, it is okay to fellowship with other believers. You say that everybody's not living as they should, not even your church-going family and friends. Well, now is the time for you to come out and be an Ezekiel. "Son of man, I have made thee a watchman unto the house of Israel; therefore hear the word at My mouth and give them warning from Me" (Ezekiel 3:17). Your job is to tell them what thus sayeth the Lord. For example, if you know that I am not living as I should, yet you refuse to tell and show me how to get it right with God, I may suffer for my sins, but He will hold you accountable as well. The blood will be on your hands. It is light's job to expose darkness, and God has called you the light of the world (Matthew 5:14).

## F. Have You Been Rejected?

Who denied you like they did Christ? Who rejected you like they did Christ? Who looked over you like they did Christ? Sometimes rejection is good because you don't need to be in situations that will bring you down. In certain circumstances, what you see or feel as rejection is God's way of keeping you from things that would lead you farther away from Him. When the world doesn't accept who you are, it is God's way of sheltering you in His everlasting arms. Rejection is also God's signal that there are areas in your life in which you need to grow. You need character and charisma just like God. If you are facing rejection, it is important, not to seek the approval of people, but to seek the presence of God. "But seek ye first the kingdom of God, and His righteousness; and all these things shall be added unto you" (Matthew 6:33). Look at what God is saying. If you seek His face, seek and read His word, and get Him in your mind, body, and soul, then He will hear from heaven and heal your land (2 Chronicles 7:14). If you just allow God to take full control and charge of your life, He will make you purer and richer in Christ. He will give you beauty for your ashes.

## G. Can You Forgive and Live?

God says that His thoughts are not our thoughts, nor are His ways our ways. "For My thoughts are not your thoughts, neither are your ways My ways,' declares the Lord," (Isaiah 55:8). When someone offends you, think about God and say, "What would Jesus do in this situation? Would He forgive? Would He seek revenge?" "Take heed to yourselves; if thy brother sin, rebuke him; and if he repent, forgive him. And if he trespass against thee seven times a day, and seven times in a day turn again to thee, saying, 'I repent,'; thou shalt forgive him" (Luke 17:3, 4). Forgive your enemy for trespassing against you. Forgive the very elect whom you trust, yet they hurt you. The more you forgive, the more God can forgive you. You might ask how you can forgive when you've been treated unfairly. How do you get healed when people have hurt you so badly? Well, your healing is in your praise. Your joy is in your praise. Your hope and understanding is in your praise. Your breakthrough is in your praise. Everything comes when you praise! Become robed in His righteousness, and see what happens. Become full of glory like Him, and see what happens. Your dark nights will become full of joy, peace, love, and understanding. You will see a different aspect of life. You will become more and more equipped to serve and walk like Him. "For bodily exercise profiteth little; but godliness is profitable unto all things, having promise of the life that now is, and of that which is to come" (1 Timothy 4:8). Don't be like those who drown their hurts in overeating and overdrinking, but turn to the Lord for comfort, "for the kingdom of God is not meat and drink; but righteousness, and peace, and joy in the Holy Ghost" (Romans 14:17). Robe yourself in the joy of the Lord that strengthens you. Arise from feeling sorry for yourself and bequest the things God has to offer you in this lifetime. Do not wait on someone's approval for what you want and feel like you need to do. Gird your loin, forgive others who have offended you and live like there is no tomorrow. Enjoy Life!

**Discussion Questions:**

1. **Do you believe that we live in a crooked and perverse world? Why or why not?**

2. **Are you alienating yourself from the world, or are you sharing the good news with the world?**

3. **Are you living what you believe?**

4. **If I follow you for a month, would I decide to follow your God, or would I change my mind and live a worldly lifestyle?**

5. **Are you wearing the full armor of God to protect yourself?**

6. **Is Jesus pleased with the way you're living right now?**

7. **Have you ever been rejected by people? Did that rejection pull you toward or away from Christ?**

**8. Are you robed in Christ's righteousness or your own self-righteousness?**

**Points to Discuss: After reading the lesson, go back and answer the questions in the lesson for an in-depth discussion.**

**Notes:**

## LESSON 29

# Do to Men What You Would Have Them Do to You

**Foundation: Matthew 7:12**

*"Therefore all things what-so-ever ye would that men should do to you, do ye even so to them: for this is the law and the prophets."*

### A. Live the Golden Rule

Even if the world is chaotic, still apply the Golden Rule to your everyday life. We are to do for others every good thing to help them reach their highest spiritual goals because this is what we would have other believers do for us. Remember: "Therefore all things whatsoever ye would that men should do to you, do ye even so to them; for this is the Law and the Prophets" (Matthew 7:12). What can you do for the upbringing of the Kingdom? What are you doing right now to make it better? Are you living a wholesome life for Christ? Have you reached your fullest potential to do His will? Are you reaching out to those who are lost and asking what you can do to make life better? Where do you stand with Christ? With Christ, all things are possible to Him that believes. "And He said, the things which are impossible with men are possible with God." Luke 18:27 Read Romans 12:1-21; focus on v. 18, "If it be possible, as much as lieth in you, live peaceably with all men."

Regardless of how people may treat you, it is your solemn duty to treat others courteously and with respect. Things may seem difficult, confusing, and overwhelming around you, but you are to stay grounded and rooted in the Word of God. You know that the Word is powerful and sharper than any two-edged sword (Hebrews 4:12); this is why it is in your best interest to stay abased when it comes to God's people. Some may seem like the very ones whom

Satan is using to follow and trample on you, but stay in the grace and solitude of the Most High. In the end, you win in Christ! Remember God sees all and knows all. Get connected in His power, and you will better be able to defeat the traps and schemes of the enemy. It's time to go the extra mile and in the direction of God's destination for what He has for you. Remember that your test is but for a moment and will develop into what you make of it as you hold on to the true and living God.

**B. Are You Seeking Recognition from God or Man?**

Do not do things to be recognized by men, but give God the glory. The Lord says if we would just do His works, He would give us a land flowing with milk and honey. To do the will of the Lord is much better than any riches, houses or land. Seek His guidance, for it is pure doctrine that is stated and sound. He is the great I AM. In Job 41:11, He says, "Who hath prevented me that I should repay him? Whatsoever is under the whole heaven is Mine." Why are we waiting, and what are we looking for? We are our own hindrance. Get up! Serve the Lord! Do what thus saith the Word! If you open the Word of God, they will come running. Everybody is tired, seeking an outlet, and looking for a breakthrough. God will hold you accountable if you do not respond to Him and do His works. We all have a purpose in life. What is yours? The sooner you seek Him, the better. Get a passion about doing good toward everyone even when they misuse and talk about you. Get a grand slam for being righteous, even when it hurts. When you do this, God will get the glory. "But we have this treasure in earthen vessels, that the excellency of the power may be of God, and not of us" (2 Corinthians 4:7).

**Discussion Questions:**

1. **Are you the type of person who does something for someone and talk about it to others?**

2. **Do you want others to do for you, but you never do anything for others but just yourself?**

3. **Do you feel like the world owes you for what you've had to go through in your past?**

4. **Do you treat everyone like they are special, or do you only do it for select ones?**

5. **Do you like hearing your name "reign" in church or at work for doing something wonderful? Why?**

6. **Do you do things out of the goodness of your heart or do you do them for recognition only? Would you still do good works if you were never recognized?**

7. **Sometimes people cry out for recognition and are never satisfied because others don't care for them. Is this you or someone you know? What word of wisdom would you give to this person or to yourself?**

8. **Are you looking for an outlet through Christ or the world?**

**Points to Discuss: After reading the lesson, go back and answer the questions in the lesson for an in-depth discussion.**

**Notes:**

# LESSON 30

# *Filthy Rags But Favor With God*

**Foundation: Haggai 2:10-19**

*"In the four and twentieth day of the ninth month, in the second year of Dairus, came the word of the Lord by Haggai the prophet, saying, 'Thus saith the Lord of hosts: ask now the priests concerning the law, saying, "If one bear holy flesh in the skirt of his garment, and with his skirt do touch bread, or pottage, or wine, or oil, or any meat, shall it be holy?" And the priests answered and said, 'No.' Then said Haggai, 'If one that is unclean by a dead body touch any of these, shall it be unclean?' And the priests answered and said, 'It shall be unclean.' Then answered Haggai, and said, 'So is this people, and so is this nation before Me, saith the Lord; and so is every work of their hands; and that which they offer there is unclean. And now, I pray you, consider from this day and upward, from before a stone was laid upon a stone in the temple of the Lord. Since those days were, when one came to a heap of twenty measures, there were but ten: when one came to the pressfat for to draw out fifty vessels out of the press, there were but twenty. I smote you with blasting and with mildew and with hail in all the labors of your hands; yet ye turned not to Me, saith the Lord. Consider now from this day and upward, from the four and twentieth day of the ninth month, even from the day that the foundation of the Lord's temple was laid, consider it. Is the seed yet in the barn? Yea, as yet the vine, and the fig tree, and the pomegranate, and the olive tree, hath not brought forth: from this day will I bless you.'"*

## A. In Need of God's Favor

As God spoke to the prophet Haggai, He laid the foundation of His precepts upon the people to recognize and honor Him; yet, their hands were unclean, and the state of their minds was defiled. Still, God blessed them. As we take a look around at the situations going on in the world today, we clearly see that Satan is busy going to and fro seeking so many people to defile, to destroy, and to make fools out of them. The more you listen to the news, the more you hear of people killing one another, of babies being sexually tainted, of older people being beaten and killed for money, or of others being violated. People, struggling to make ends meet, are killing one another for money, food, and clothing. The world is in a state of depression and shock. There are wars and rumors of wars that are never ending; yet, God still is in control. He still is able to bless His people, but do we believe? Do we believe He is merciful to forgive and mighty to bless and to save? We sit back, criticize, and complain about that which somebody else is doing, but we, ourselves, are doing nothing to make that person and the situation better. People have become so complacent and comfortable. They have become more into themselves than into pleasing God. It is more of a "me, my, mine, and I" generation where whatever is said and done is okay, even if it is wrong. Isaiah says that our self-righteous works are like filthy rags to God (64:6). If our self-righteous works are dirty before the Almighty, what is our wickedness like to Him? We, as Israel was, are in desperate times; we need His favor again.

## B. God Knows the True "You"

God knows your thoughts before you think it. He has all power in His hands. For He said in His word, "Humble yourselves therefore under the mighty hand of God, that He may exalt you in due time: Casting all your care upon Him; for He careth for you." 1 Peter 5:6-7. The battle is not yours it is the Lord. If He brings you to a problem/situation, He will bring you through it. It is not for you to decipher through and decide what you will do. He wants you to give it and leave it with him. You are to cast *all* of your cares on Him because He cares for you. God said the defiled men are sick in their own glory. He is a jealous God. He wants to get the honor and praise. He is our comforter and keeper.

Do you not understand that when you are in a position of authority, higher league/member, manager, any person with a job title, pew keeper, secretary, usher, choir member, deacon, minister of music, anybody, you are held in high accountability for your soul and the soul of others around you. Once we taint with sin, we become defiled and unclean. Just praying and asking God for repentance to clear you is not enough. With all due respect, you must become what you want to be through Christ. Walk the walk by reading and understanding and truly living according to the word. If you keep feeding your spirit by reading the word, God will draw you closer and closer to him. Even if you do not understand what you are reading, the spirit does. It will bring it back to your recollection as time permits. You will better be able to understand it by and by. Understand this, signs and wonders shall follow but they will not follow if you are not reading. In all of your getting, get understanding. Follow and obey the word to receive favor with God.

The problem with most people is the Bible is not entertaining enough to them. Pray first and ask the Lord to help with reading and understanding His mysteries. Once you read daily and eat the word, make it a part of your daily routines by eating, sleeping and breathing it, than you will be able to understand what the word of the Lord is saying that is revealed to you. You must pray and read, read and pray, but all in all, you must be sincere. What does it profit a man to gain the world and lose His soul? What will it profit you to walk around daily talking like you got it going on and living a ragged and messed up life? What does it profit for you to pretend that you are living right, when you are caught up in your mess and in your stuff? You need JESUS! God sees all and He knows all. He desires for your filthy rags to be turned into favor if you abide in Him.

**C. Get It Right to Receive Favor**

Churches, relatives, friends, and people, it is time for us to get it right with God! You will never be able to have true comfort and ease if you are not living right. You see, God wants a vessel that is unspotted and clean. He wants a world that is not wrinkled, spotted, and living and wallowing in sin. He wants humility, not those who walk around as if they are "all that and a bag of chips," too together for God but so messed up they cannot approach God. You cannot come into His presence and His glory any kind of way, pretending that everything is alright. He wants you, with all of your mess, to get it right with Him. Remember, He is an all-knowing God. He knows your thoughts, even before you think it. He knows your actions, your gestures, and your signs; He knows the ragged and unclean you. God said He will wipe away every one of our tears if we would seek Him first. He will reveal the mysteries of this world. You won't have to rob Peter to pay Paul. You won't have to pretend that everything is wonderful when, really, it is torn up, ragged, messed up, and tainted. It is no fun living a lie.

### D. Are You Giving In to Sex as the Cure-all?

God has a destiny for everybody, if only you would trust and believe in Him. The answer is not always in sex. Regardless of how and what predicament it will put you in, it seems to always be the answer to those who do not believe. Many people, but especially women, would rather seek acceptance through sex than to accept God's favor. "I know I'm flawed; I know I messed up, but if he sleeps with me, that must make me okay. It must mean I'm alright." Men buy cars, flaunt money, or take pills to make themselves more pleasurable to women, but sex cannot take the place of God's favor and acceptance of you. Even for those who are willing to live a homosexual lifestyle because they've been rejected by the opposite sex, God's favor cannot be replaced. Try as we might, Church, neither is His favor earned nor is His favor replaced. We need God's favor! We need God's mercy! And He is ready to show His loving kindness, even now. Although this world is corrupt and defiled, God still Loves us.

### E. Give In to God

Understand this: it may seem alright for the outward appearance to be well-groomed while the inside is torn up, but in the end, where will you be? Are you standing in a dark spot thinking that it is alright and that nobody really knows what is going on because you're such a *nice person*, a *deacon* in the church, a *minister* in the church, a *choir member*, or an *usher*? People know that you are a *nice person,* so it is okay for you to have a mistress or significant other. It is okay for you to sneak and date somebody else's husband or wife. It is okay because you're not doing your dirt all the time anyway; it's only every now and then that you "slip," "stumble," or "take a break to build your testimony." Guess what, wrong answer. When you entertain the thoughts, trickery, and schemes of the enemy, everybody knows, and it is no longer a secret.

Church folks who are doing the same things as the "street committee," are no different than the street committee. When you are in the church and a part of the Kingdom of God, you have to give account for everything that you do. Everything you do and say is connected to every individual part of your household and church family. Every error you make not only affects you but also affects the next person. I cannot go around pretending that everything is alright when I have skeletons in my closet, pornography under my bed, weaknesses beyond control, and fantasies of things that should not be. Remember: "…for as he thinketh in his heart, so is he" (Proverbs 23:7). You cannot think it and lust after it and it not become a part of you. It is the same as actually doing it. It is hard to walk the walk and to talk the talk truthfully when you want to enjoy the pleasures of the world and still be a part of God's Kingdom. God is a jealous God, and He wants us to give Him all the glory, all the honor, and all the praise. If we are praising and worshipping our own acts of disobedience, then we are not bound to God.

He created man in His image, but it is up to man to live for Him, through Him, and in Him. Ask the Lord to live in you and to have His way in you. The more you search and seek the dynamics of His image in your life, the more you will see a change for the better. It is hard at first, but the more you seek God, and the more you seek to read, to understand, and to abide in His Word and will, the easier it will be. God wants us to be like Him. God will settle you and help you to understand the foul spirit that is within when you seek Him. He will show you yourself in the mirror. He will expose the inner man. It's not just by chance that you're not happy with your spouse or significant other. It is not them; it is you. You do not have a personal relationship with God. If you ask Him in all sincerity and put yourself to the side, then will you be better able to see the promises He has for you. The reason you are not where you think you should be is because *you* are trying to fix it and work it out. The only thing you are doing is spinning your wheels but not moving. You will never get out of the rut you are in unless you come out of yourself and get into God. He will give you the joy that no man can steal or take away. You will not feel the same. The thought of fornicating and committing adultery will become a stench in your nostrils. Anything of which He is not a part will finally fade away and disappear. He has to be at the center, root, and foundation of everything and in every part of your life. Let Him use you for real, and see the changes that will come to pass. You have not because you ask not, or you ask amiss and use it for your own glory. It will never work. Come to Jesus while you have time, and allow Him to whisper the sweet nothings in your ear. Talk to Him, and discuss all of your problems and situations. You will be amazed at how things really will work in your favor!

**Discussion Questions:**

1. **Are you in need of God's favor for your life?**

2. **Do you recognize your areas of weakness but God has favored it?**

3. **Do you see in yourself what others see in you?**

4. **Do you feel that by reading and obeying the Word will allow you to obtain favor with God?**

5. **Are you falling prey to the Word or the world?**

6. **Do you feel like sex is a cure-all and replaces God in your life? Why or Why not?**

7. **Do you have a personal relationship with God that demonstrates His favor in your life?**

8. **Are you living with filthy rags and seeking to obtain a relationship with God?**

9. **Whose image are you walking in?**

10. **Are your hands unclean but God is still blessing you? What are you doing to make it right in the sight of the Lord?**

**Points to Discuss: After reading the lesson, go back and answer the questions in the lesson for an in-depth discussion.**

**Notes:**

## LESSON 31

# *Greater Possessions Are Stored Up for You*

**Foundation: Deuteronomy 3:16-18**

*"And unto the Reubenites and unto the Gadites I gave from Gilead even unto the river Arnon half the valley, and the border even unto the river Jabbok, which is the border of the children of Ammon; The plain also, and Jordan, and the coast thereof, from Chinereth even unto the sea of the plain, even the Salt Sea, under Ashdoth-pisgah eastward. And I commanded you at that time, saying, 'The LORD your God hath given you this land to possess it: ye shall pass over armed before your brethren the children of Israel, all that are meet for the war.'"*

### A. Greater Blessing in Store

Your latter will be greater. God is providing the land to possess, but you must follow the rules according to His will. There are circumstances and situations beyond our control, but we must fast and pray for answers to be revealed. There are ways in which you can obtain the promise but you must be obedient to the Word. There are circumstances that may seem grim, but just hold on to God's unchanging hands, and you will see the promise come to pass. Weeping may endure for a night but joy comes in the morning (Psalm 30:5).

Rest is what we seek, but God says to seek Him in all of our doings. The more we pray, the more He will reveal situations and ways to prosper. The land of possession is what He already has in His master plan. In order to acquire it, we must be ready to follow His rules. There are ways that seem tiresome and grim to man, but they are not foolishness to God. People say that they want the promises, but they do not want to experience what it takes to get them. There are challenges in this world that will try to keep us from seeing things God's way, but in order to become a beacon of light, one must be willing to give up the lifestyle that is currently pleasing to him in order to do what's pleasing to *Him*.

God has a plan that is even greater than what you currently possess. His plan is deeper and less complicated. God will provide, if only we wait for it. He who will come, shall come, and will not tarry. When the possessions come, don't be weary in your well-doing. Put God to the test, and watch Him bring greater things to pass. He has so much to release, and He is waiting for you to retrieve it. Open your mind, heart, body, and soul for Him to release it, and flourish in His giving.

### B. Belonging to the Kingdom and Having Its Mentality

"But these are they of which ye shall not eat; the eagle, and the ossifrage, and the ospray, And the glede, and the kite, and the vulture after his kind, And every raven after his kind, And the owl, and the night hawk, and the cuckow, and the hawk after his kind, The little owl, and the great owl, and the swan, And the pelican, and the gier eagle, and the cormorant. And the stork, and the heron after her kind, and the lapwing, and the bat. And every creeping thing that flieth is unclean unto you: they shall not be eaten. But of all clean fowls ye may eat. Ye shall not eat of anything that dieth of itself: thou shalt give it unto the stranger that is in thy gates, that he may eat it; or thou mayest sell it unto an alien: for thou art a holy people unto the Lord thy God. Thou shalt not seethe a kid in his mother's milk. Thou shalt truly tithe all the increase of thy seed, that the field bringeth forth year by year. And thou shalt eat before the Lord thy God, in the place which He shall choose to place His name there, the tithe of thy corn, of thy wine, and of thine oil, and the firstlings of thy herds and of thy flocks; that thou mayest learn to fear the Lord thy God always. And if the way be too long for thee, so that thou art not able to carry it; or if the place be too far from thee, which the Lord thy God shall choose to set His name there, when the Lord thy God hath blessed thee: Then shalt thou turn it into money, and bind up the money in thine hand, and shalt go unto the place which the Lord thy God shall choose: And thou shalt bestow that money for whatsoever thy soul lusteth after, for oxen, or for sheep, or for wine, or for strong drink, or for whatsoever thy soul desireth: and thou shalt eat there before the Lord thy God, and thou shalt rejoice, thou, and thine household, And the Levite that is within thy gates; thou shalt not forsake him; for he hath no part nor inheritance with thee. At the end of three years thou shalt bring forth all the tithe of thine increase the same year, and shalt lay it up within thy gates: And the Levite, (because he hath no part nor inheritance with thee,) and the stranger, and the fatherless, and the widow, which are within thy gates, shall come, and shall eat and be satisfied; that the Lord thy God may bless thee in all the work of thine hand which thou doest" (Deuteronomy 14:12-29).

By obeying the rules of God, we carry out the Kingdom mentality. As indicated above in Deuteronomy alone indicates obedience and following through with the instructions of God. Anyone can have the riches of life if they are obedient to the will of God and his blessings shall overflow. Jesus is the Kingdom and by us following Him, we are following and adhering to the Realm. Just think, if we follow Him, He'll give us the desires of our heart. "The life is more than meat, and the body is more than raiment. Consider the ravens; for they neither sow nor reap, which neither have storehouse nor barn; and God feedeth them: how much more are ye better than the fowls? And which of you with taking thought can add to His stature one cubit? If ye then be not able to do that thing which is least, why take ye thought for the rest? Consider the lilies how they grow: they toil not, they spin not; and yet I say unto you, that Solomon in all his glory was not arrayed like one of these. If then God so clothe the grass, which is today in the field, and tomorrow is cast into the oven; how much more will He clothe you, O ye of little faith? And seek not ye what ye shall eat, or what ye shall drink, neither be ye of doubtful mind. For all these things do the nations of the world seek after: and your Father knoweth that ye have need of these things. But rather seek ye the kingdom of God; and all these things shall be added unto you. Fear not, little flock; for it is your Father's good pleasure to give you the kingdom. Sell that ye have, and give alms; provide yourselves bags which wax not old, a treasure in the heavens that faileth not, where no thief approacheth, neither moth corrupteth. For where your treasure is, there will your heart be also" (Luke 12:23-34).

We are a part of the head and not the tail. We are above and not beneath. We belong to God not Idols, Baptist, Hindu, or Buddha but God. We are to have a Kingdom mentality and not that of the world. If we continue to try to satisfy men and race against time, then we will never win; meaning that if we do the works of the Kingdom, time will satisfy itself. God wants us to enjoy the fruit of our inheritance. He said that the earth belongs to Him. You have not because you ask not or ask amiss. God wants us to enjoy His fruits, His inheritance, and the things He brought forth to the end. Life is short; then, you die. Ten years from now, will we be able to say that we enjoyed our children while they were young? Will we be able to say that we are enjoying our parenthood because we are spending a lot of quality time with our children? Will we be able to say that we remember when our children did this, that, and the other, or will we say, "I wish I would have been there more"? Will we say, "I wish I would've had more time to do this, that, and the other"? God wants us to stop, to slow down, and to smell the roses. In the United States, we have not had a chance to do much of anything as a family because of time. We are in a rush, always; and the more we race against time, the more we will lose.

Sure, everybody wants to be rich. Everybody would love to have the material things in life and to receive the blessings. I often think about the rich – the fortunate ones who get the inheritance and still share the blessings of God and enjoy life. Life is abundance in itself which no one is able to erase. When you have a Kingdom mentality, everybody in the household buys into the business and pleasures of the Lord. When you take care of business for God, He will take care of you. When you grant your worship, time, and life to and for Christ, He will make everything alright. You will not have to worry about paying for pleasures and not paying your bills. You will not have to rob Peter to pay Paul. You will have a stream and flow of revenue coming in to satisfy the needs and wants of the household. God is the Father of peace. He gives His elect the desires of their hearts. The land is yours! The possessions are yours! "But seek ye first the Kingdom of God, and His righteousness; and all these things shall be added unto you" (Matthew 6:33).

Everything can be claimed by the abundance and overflow of your capital through God. You will be able to lay claim of things you desire. You will have a better understanding of the economy according to God. You will have a glimpse of the reality of life through Christ. He is rich indeed. If my God is rich in houses and land, so am I. Seek Him for guidance in your finances and your desires, and see Him grant you all the things of which you have need. God wants us to depend on Him for the things we need in life. He will grant it.

**Discussion Questions:**

1. **Whose mentality do you possess?**

2. **Do you think everything you do is right, even when it falls outside of God's ordinances?**

3. **Are you living life in abundance through Christ?**

4. **Are you living a life full of joy in Christ?**

5. **Are you stopping to spend quality time with family, friends, and yourself?**

6. **Are you spending quality time with God?**

7. **Are you enjoying the fruit of your labor or someone else's?**

8. **Are you racing against time or Christ?**

**Points to Discuss: After reading the lesson, go back and answer the questions in the lesson for an in-depth discussion.**

**Notes:**

## LESSON 32

# *Let Us Make a Joyful Noise Unto the Lord*

**Foundation: Psalm 95:1-9**

> *"O COME, let us sing unto the LORD: let us make a joyful noise to the rock of our salvation. Let us come before His presence with thanksgiving, and make a joyful noise unto Him with psalms. For the Lord is a great God, and a great King above all gods. In His hand are the deep places of the earth: the strength of the hills is His also. The sea is his, and He made it: and His hands formed the dry land. O come, let us worship and bow down: let us kneel before the LORD our maker. For He is our God; and we are the people of His pasture, and the sheep of His hand. Today if ye will hear His voice, Harden not your heart, as in the provocation, and as in the day of temptation in the wilderness: When your father tempted me, proved me, and saw my work."*

Do you have days when you would like to shout on the rooftop? Are there moments when you would like to scream because life is so difficult and confusing that you do not know what to do? Do you have times when everything seems grim and out of control? Be reassured you can turn to Jesus. Sometimes God will place that significant person in your life with whom you can relate. It seems difficult and less secure to release your problems to others when you are accustomed to being the problem solver yourself, but God will place the right person there just for you. No, I am not saying that it will be someone else's spouse or significant other. You do not have to define a relationship with someone based on sex. Some things can be discussed and determined as mutual friends. Men may try to get wisdom from women under the disguise of "mutual friends," but their true intentions are to get closer sexually. So, instead of putting yourself in these harsh and cruel predicaments, rely on the one and true God our Savior.

It is okay to check with God about your problems or situations. Make a joyful noise unto Him when you feel like you are in despair and have no way out. Pray aloud and shout with a voice of triumph unto Him. Tell Him all about your problems and circumstances. Make God your primary contact for everything. He can and He will make everything alright. He wants us to make a joyful noise unto Him so that He can get all of the glory, the honor, and the praise. God is ever seeking us to worship Him and to turn our attention to Him. He is passionate about His people. He wants us to trust in Him and Him alone. When you make an angry shout out to Him, He knows. When you shout it out over the rooftop out of anger, He will turn it into a joyful noise. He will turn your anguish into tears of joy. He will turn your lonely heart and heart of despair into a heart of joy, peace, longsuffering and pride in Him. God does not want us to feel anguished and disappointed. He wants us to have a yearning for Him. He wants our desires to be fulfilled in His sight. He is a precious and caring God. Look to Him as the Author and Finisher of your faith. He will clean up what you have messed up when you make that joyful noise unto Him. Look to Him for determination and authentication. He will give you direction, guidance, gratitude and elevation. When you are feeling in despair and cheated, He will give you fulfillment and joy.

Make a joyful noise unto Him with a heart of thanksgiving and joy. Even when you are not feeling like it is going to be okay, just know that God is not a man that He should lie, and He is faithful to keep His promises. He who will come, shall come, and will not tarry. Wait, I say, on the Lord! He is your buckler and your shield. He is your sounding board when you want to shout it out for the world to hear!

**Discussion Questions:**

1. **Who is the person you're more apt to call on when times are hard?**

2. **Have you established a relationship with God, and can you communicate with Him?**

3. **Are you certain that you are welcome in His Kingdom?**

4. **When you call on the name of the Lord, does He answer? If so, how and when does He respond? If not, why do you think He's not responding?**

5. **Do you look to God with a heart of gratitude?**

6. **Is God truly directing your path in life? Why or why not?**

7. **Are you proud of where you are in Christ during this walk? Why or why not?**

**Points to Discuss: After reading the lesson, go back and answer the questions in the lesson for an in-depth discussion.**

**Notes:**

Congratulations on completing *Divine Release*! I hope and pray that it was helpful and that it allowed you to search within yourself for where God has you and where He is taking you in life. Continue to embrace one another while you go through this milestone. Love unconditionally, and give from your heart. Watch the glory of God manifest and mold you into what God has already ordained.

Be blessed in the name of the Lord Jesus Christ!

# ACKNOWLEDGMENT

Now that this book has been released, I pray that it reaches the hearts and souls for whom it's destined. I would like to extend a special and warm thank you to my husband, Lawrence, for encouraging and coaching me to finish this book, which has been placed on and off the shelf for years. Special thanks is extended to my daughters, Lauryn and Leah, for watching and hearing the developing phases of what has been poured out to so many. I especially thank my mother, Lannie Bennett, for reading sections, for never being able to put it down, and for providing feedback as if she were in a group discussion. I also thank my mother-in-law, Geraldine Kearse Cherry, for always encouraging and motivating me.

I thank my niece, Ebony Greene, Lead Editor of KingPen Editors (www.kingpeneditors.com; kingpeneditors@gmail.com), for revising, editing, and proofreading the entire book from start to finish. She, too, was dedicated in seeing it through. Without her input and feedback, it wouldn't have reached the final phase. She enjoyed the material and had a hard time putting it down. Praise God!

I would also like to thank my sister, Wanda; brother-in-law, Morris; and niece, Tamika, for aiding me with researching scriptures while in the writing phase. They were readily available at any time when I was dissecting parts of what God had me to say as it related to the spoken word. Special thanks are extended to my brothers, Michael and McArthur Jr.; and my nephew Morris Jr. for making it easier for me to have a story.

A warm gratitude is extended to family and friends for encouraging and praying for me. Much gratitude is extended to Pastor George F. Edge and Rev. Fer-Rell Malone Sr. for their spiritual guidance and teaching the word so boldly. Pastor Edge you pushed me into my destiny for the Lord.

Finally, I would like to express my deepest gratitude to my God and Savior, Jesus Christ. Without Him, I am not able to do anything; but with Him, all things are possible. I believe He'll take me through another phase with something special for His elect people.

It has been a pleasure!

# REFERENCE

*The King James Study Bible: King James Version.* Nashville: Thomas Nelson, 1988. Print.